Make money fr
home recording

This book is dedicated to all my tuition and recording students, past, present and future.

Clive Brooks
The Sound Workshop
Southampton

Make money from home recording

Clive Brooks

PC Publishing
4 Brook Street
Tonbridge
Kent TN9 2PJ

First published 1989

© Clive Brooks

ISBN 1 870775 25 2

British Library Cataloguing in Publication Data

Brookes, Clive
  Make money from home recording.
  1. Recording studios, Home-based
  small firms. Management
  I. Title
  621. 389 '3' 068

  ISBN 1-870775-25-2

Phototypesetting by Just Words Ltd, Ellen Street, Portslade.
Printed and bound by LR Printing Services, Manor Royal,
Crawley, West Sussex

Contents

1 Setting up a studio

It's not easy to persuade family, friends and neighbours that a recording studio within your home is a good idea. However, there are many different options open to you, and for many of the moneymaking schemes in this book you won't need a studio at all. Instead, you can transport your equipment to your clients instead. But there's no doubt about it, a place to record at home *is* useful, and it need not cause much disruption.

The ideal situation would be a recording room that can be divided into two sections: The studio itself, where the musicians actually play, and a separate control room with a glass window in the dividing wall, so that the engineer (you) can see through into your studio.

As a home recordist, you'll probably run into noise problems, either from neighbours, or other members of the household who might not like hearing the same bit of music 28 times in succession, whilst you struggle to get an overdub right. It's also likely that you'll have to make compromises with your studio construction too. But have you ever considered utilizing the garage? It's just the right size, often situated away from the house, and can easily be soundproofed (see Figure 1.3).

Planning your studio

How you plan your studio depends largely on what you're planning to record, and whether most of your moneymaking sessions will be on location, or situated in your studio (in Chapter 3 you'll find ideas suitable for both). If you opt for the former, then all you really need is a place to store your recording equipment and accessories when not in use. Noise problems, when you do occasionally embark upon some home-based recording, can easily be solved by simply plugging

1

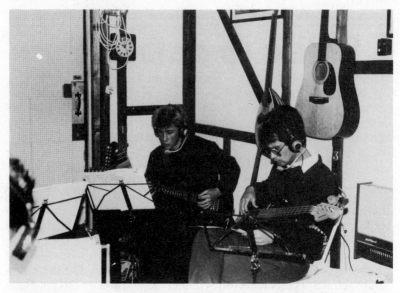

Figure 1.1 Guitar playing author in his studio built in the garden from a converted garage linked to a summer room. The soundproofing is explained later in this chapter

Figure 1.2 The author in the control room of his home studio

whatever you're using direct in to the mixing desk. This has the added bonus of making the acoustics of the recording room much less important.

From the home-based point of view, you'll probably find yourself in one of four situations. The first is where your friendly family give you access to two adjoining rooms for recording. Situation number two is where you have just one large room — such as a garage. The third is where part of a room can be temporarily put to use, and finally number four, where the only space you've got is a wardrobe in a bedroom!

Adjoining rooms

Having two rooms gives you the chance to set up a 'real studio'. You can achieve excellent isolation between musicians and engineer this way. But, unless you can knock a hole in the wall, some kind of intercom system will be required between the two areas. You'll also need to remember that you'll need extra-long runs of cable, feeding microphones in the recording room to the mixer in the control room. Although all this sounds wonderful, there are disadvantages—especially if you're working alone: you can't be in two places at once, and you'll need to switch on the tape recorder, then rush into the other room and pick up an instrument or whatever. This problem is made worse when you come to overdubs—you switch on, rush into the other room, only to find that the track's already started, or the monitoring is too quiet. Then, when you do finally make a recording, you notice that the recording level was either far too low, making the recording hissy, or far too high, resulting in distortion. You could argue that all this could be solved with use of an assistant. But they're never around when you need them, and using someone else on your moneymaking schemes will mean that they'll want a cut of your profits!

A single room

Although less glamorous, this situation is better suited to the money-making home recordist. The bigger the room that you can use the better—bigger rooms provide natural reverberation if they're empty, and this could save you buying an electrical unit. However, there are drawbacks associated with adding reverb naturally at source. The main one is that you're stuck with it on the recording, whether you like it or not. To be honest, I've always found that a dry, unprocessed sound is best for most of the time—it's certainly best for mixing down—an echoey room can be a nightmare—you compensate for it and get a good sound, then you play the tape in another room and it sounds horrendous. If possible, you want to go for a cross between the two.

Professional studios have elaborate wall structures made of fibreglass-filled boards which are both expensive and a little too drastic for most homes. An alternative is to line the walls with thick carpet hung from battens. This can be removed when an echoey sound is required, and replaced when it isn't. It won't look particularly elegant, but it will work — and it won't damage the room much either. A good sound dampener for the ceiling is a piece of fabric suspended over the entire area.

As well as general soundproofing treatments, you'll often need separation between individual instrument sounds which are being recorded simultaneously. The best way to achieve this is with baffles. These are large plates made of thick wood, with panels of sound absorbent material glued to them. you simply plonk these down between drums and amps to minimize leakage (one microphone picking up unwanted sound from another instrument close by).

The reason that leakage is such a bad thing these days, is that with multitrack, each different sound is recorded on a separate channel, and if some of one sound spills onto another track, then all control during mixdown disappears. For example, say you want to fade the drums out on a part of the mix, but some of the drum sound has spilled onto the bass track during recording. You fade the drums out, but they can still be heard through the bass. this is even more of a problem if you've added an effect to the bass track, as suddenly the drums will start to sound strange. Too much leakage defeats the object of having instruments or sounds on separate tracks in the first place.

If you don't want to build some baffles, then you could separate parts of the room by simply curtaining them off from others. This works in much the same way. It's best to use the plastic 'Swish' type curtain track — metal ones tend to rattle during recordings. As a garage is a probable option for many home recordists, there follows a detailed explanation of how to build cost-effective soundproofing into one.

Soundproofing

Whilst it is virtually impossible to completely prevent sound travel-

4

ling through a structure such as a garage without severely limiting its already small size, the following soundproofing idea will drastically minimize noise, and in most cases render your recording acceptable to neighbours.

The biggest problem is that of low frequencies, for instance, a bass drum thud. The structure shown here has the effect of breaking down soundwaves by dispersing them through sheets of perforated hardboard. Following this they are absorbed by high density mineral fibre slabs, an air gap, a layer of roofing felt, and finally the actual concrete garage wall. As you can imagine, not a great deal of the sound remains (see Figure 1.3).

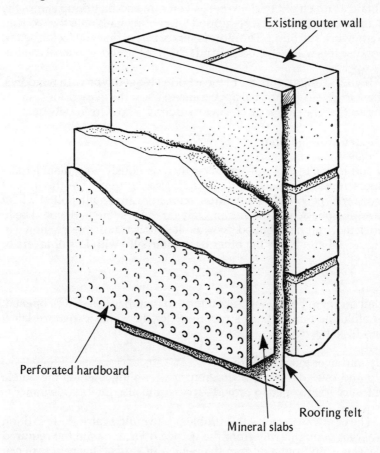

Figure 1.3 An effective method of soundproofing

Side door
Option 1
If you are lucky enough to have a side door on your garage then the first option is to brick up your existing main garage doorway with concrete blocks. These needn't be tied into the existing wall, and as they are not load bearing, do not require a foundation; you can build directly off of the concrete floor. At a later date this wall can easily be demolished to return the garage back to its original purpose.

Option 2
If you don't want to do anything as drastic as this then you should obtain as much old thick carpet as you can, and fix this up across the main entrance, using large-headed felt roofing nails onto the wooden framework surround. The more layers of carpet that you fix the better, because this will be the point from which the sound will most eagerly escape.

If your garage doors are of the wooden hinged type with windows, then, to preserve external appearances, black the glass prior to starting so that the carpet or blockwork doesn't show from outside.

Hinged wooden doors
Option 1
If you haven't got a side entrance, then obviously your main garage doors must still function to afford access. If you have the hinged wooden type, opening outwards, one door can remain bolted whilst the other one acts as the entrance. By far the best method would be to brick up behind the bolted door, as close to it as possible, as shown in Figure 1.4 and cover the other door internally with lots of layers of carpet.

Option 2
Nail carpet to both doors separately, so that they can still be opened, or build the same type of structure as for the walls, (explained later) and fit to the doors.

Up and over garage doors
Up and over doors are a different matter altogether, as the whole entrance has to open to provide access, and also internal clearance is required.

The best way to tackle this problem is to build a false stud partition wall, far enough away from the garage door to obtain the required clearance, and put a door in it, opening inwards. This new wall can then be soundproofed in common with the others.

Garage door (bolted)

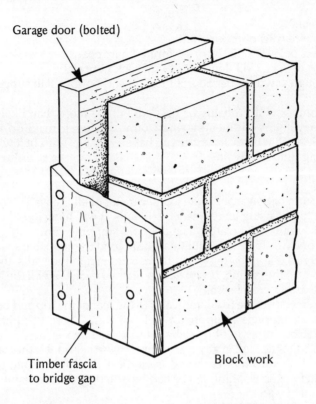

Timber fascia
to bridge gap

Block work

Figure 1.4 soundproofing the garage door

Unfortunately you are going to lose some precious space, but short of constructing a side entrance, there's not much choice. Even the smallest garage should still provide ample space to house your recording equipment and you, though.

The walls
Once the access problems are sorted out, you can turn your attention to the walls. The figures following are based on a standard garage size of 5 x 2.5m.

Ingredients
6 ten metre rolls of roofing felt
16 sheets of 2400 x 1200mm perforated hardboard
70 slabs of 80kg/M3 density mineral rock fibre slabs
40m rough sawn timber 50 x 50mm top and bottom slab supports

More timber will probably be needed, but it's more than likely that you'll have some oddments laying around. It's best to make do, where possible, with whatever timber you have available, most of it will end up being hidden anyway.

Method
Fix a 25mm batten around the top perimeter of all the walls. Then fix the felt to this using large-headed felt nails. It will hang loosely away from the wall, and create a useful sound-stopping 25mm air gap. A bigger one would be ideal but this would limit the available space too much. Fix a 50mm batten to the floor, 50mm from the walls, then do the same on the ceiling. If you have a pitched roof, then fix the batten to the existing crossbeams.

Wooden struts are fixed vertically to the rear of the top and bottom battens at intervals of approximately 600mm. These uprights will support the mineral fibre slabs. Notice that the structure is not connected to the wall in any way. This is to further inhibit the transfer of sound. Ensure that each end is supported with a strong 50mm upright. Further isolation can be had by isolating all of the joints with rubber.

Insert mineral fibre slabs into the wooden structure. These slabs can be cut to size easily, as required, using a domestic bread knife. The work area does tend to become very dusty, no matter how careful you are, and I found myself coughing and spluttering from the disgusting mineral fibre dust. Looking back, I think that the purchase of a face mask will save time, temper and health — not necessarily in that order!

Similar wooden struts are fixed in front of the mineral slabs, as in Figure 1.5.

A rebate is made here to ensure that everything finishes flush with the top and bottom battens. Saw the perforated hardboard sheets to size and fit them to the top and bottom battens with large headed nails. Ensure that the sheets join on an upright. Boards can be further fixed to the uprights using countersunk head woodscrews. The uprights can be sited through the holes in the hardboard. For appearance, you could fit a skirting board, make up a timber architrave around the door and cover all the hardboard joins with a suitable beading. A similar structure fitted to any entrances would make them just as acoustically efficient.

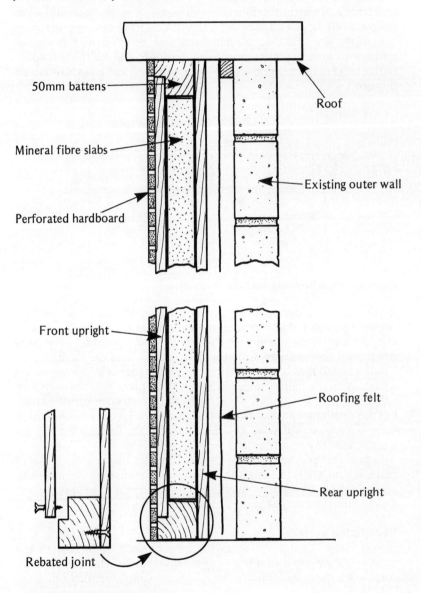

Figure 1.5 Wall soundproofing

The ceiling

The ceiling structure is similar to the walls. If you have a flat roof then the chances are that the supporting crossmembers will be visible. If you have a pitched roof then this will certainly be the case, unless of course a ceiling has already been fitted. You have two options.

Remove any existing plasterboard and proceed as follows, or remove an area big enough to work through, and fill the loft space with a layer of the mineral wool before replacing any boards removed (Figure 1.6).

Ceiling insulation

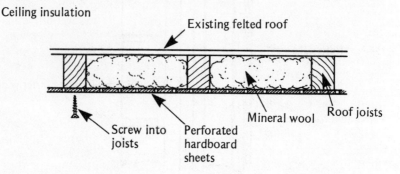

Figure 1.6 Filling the ceiling void with mineral wool

If you decide to start from scratch you will achieve a more effective finished product. If you plan to work alone then you should make a support known as a deadman's prop of suitable height, as the large hardboard sheets are really difficult to handle, and can easily tear.
Cut the hardboard to size ensuring that all of the sheets terminate on a joist. With the help of an assistant, or your prop, nail the sheets up using large headed nails. It's best not to nail directly through the holes. Fill the resultant space above as you go with a layer of mineral fibre slabs. This time protective goggles as well as the facemask really are a must, take my word for it!

Repeat this process for the whole ceiling, leaving one sheet out of place if you wish to install the following ventilation system. Nail planed timber mouldings over the joins to improve the appearance, and to eliminate any sagging in the hardboard.

Ventilation system

If you intend to use the room for long periods, especially in hot weather, then you'll find that it gets really stuffy. This can be overcome with the installation of the following simple ventilation:

Materials
Sound attenuator
Ceiling extractor fan
One metre of 200mm flexible ducting
External wall grille

The sound attenuator is a device similar to an exhaust pipe silencer. It is a metal tube with a perforated inner face. Sandwiched between this face and the outer casing is some mineral fibre. The acoustic principle used is identical to the one that we've just built for our walls and ceiling. This is the most important part of the ventilation system.

Fit the external grille to the outside wall of the garage. For simplicity, try to mount it on the wooden fascia board if you have one. Then, connect a short length of ducting between the grille and the sound attenuator — a simple push-fit usually. It's advisable to keep all the ductwork as short as possible for maximum airflow.

Measure and cut the final sheet of perforated hardboard, and mount the extractor fan in it. Connect up another length of flexible ducting to the other end of the attenuator, and the fan itself. Connect the fan up to an electricity supply, and fit the final hardboard sheet into place. This sheet will act as a support for the attenuator which is hidden above it (Figure 1.7)

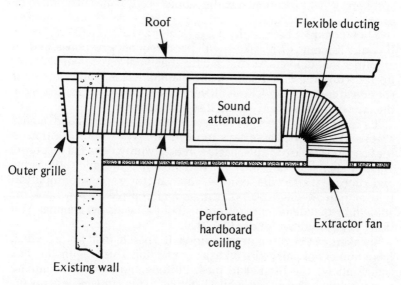

Figure 1.7 Ventilation is desirable — especially in the summer!

Temporary accommodation

If you're not able to oust the family car from its home, then you're probably going to be faced with one of the next two situations.

Set up in the corner of the living room; there's not much you can do about acoustics here, but putting a few big pillows and cushions in the room, and draping a few sheets around when you set up to record, does make for a slightly deader sound. More important considerations are to ensure that you remove any ornaments etc. that could rattle — and don't forget loud clocks either!

With your recording gear simply stowed in a wardrobe, you don't really have a studio room at all, and it's best to handle solo recordings exclusively, or work on location. The best idea is to monitor through headphones, but do buy a pair with as accurate and uncoloured a sound as possible. Specialist hi-fi shops should be helpful. Expect to pay £50 plus for a suitable set.

Monitoring

Although headphones are sometimes essential, if noise isn't too much of a problem, it's always nice to be able to hear your recordings over speakers. What I mentioned earlier about headphones needing to be uncoloured and accurate sounding goes for speaker and amplifier combinations too. Technically this is known as having a flat response. If you're listening on speakers with poor frequency response, and an amplifier that delivers too much bass, then your recordings will end up reflecting these faults. To make matters worse, you'll mix your sounds to compensate. This is all very fine until your client plays the the tape on their system — and it sounds terrible!

It's best to visit a specialist hi-fi store to audition some good quality amps and speakers. These days, most amps have a central position on the bass and treble controls that theoretically provides a flat response. Go for something plain and basic without any of the fancy little lights and knobs that affect the sound — you want pure accurate amplification, not an all-singing-all-dancing super-boosted racket. Look for something that delivers an output of about 25 watts per channel. You don't need anything louder than that.

Speakers can be difficult to audition. It's best to visit a store which has a number of pairs wire up to a comparator. This is a junction box which allows the listener to push buttons and instantly compare various different speakers whilst listening to the same piece of music. Without a comparator, you'll have to wait while the salesman disconnects the speakers you're listening to, and connects up the pair that you want to hear next. So what? Well, by the time the new pair are up and running, you've forgotten what the last pair sounded like! The ear soon becomes accustomed to new sounds. The only way to differentiate and make an informed choice is by instant comparison — don't let anyone tell you any different.

Wiring up

In the excitement of getting gear out of the box and starting to use it, many people forget to give much thought to actually wiring equipment up properly. 'Just plug it in and get going,' is a commonly heard philosophy. Whilst this can work in the short term, it can cause problems later — problems that are difficult and tedious to rectify.

Mains cables carry lots of noise with the electricity. Strange signals ride along the wire with the electrical current and get into your equipment. These can cause unwanted buzzes — you'll know what I mean if you've ever tried to record in a room that has a light-dimmer switch fitted. Strip lighting is a menace too, so avoid both in your recording studio.

Proper sockets are also very important, and should all be fused according to manufacturer's recommendations. It's vital to make sure that all earth connections are correctly made, both from a safety point of view, and because bad connections can cause unwanted hum. To save the expense of engaging an electrician to fit extra sockets, buy an extension lead terminating in a line of four sockets. But make sure that the wall outlet can handle the power that the four sockets will draw. Electricity coming from the wall shouldn't be simply something you take for granted. It has tremendous power, and can be deadly!

Some equipment doesn't have an earth wire leading to the plug. On such equipment, you will often find a terminal labelled 'ground' on the back. This should be connected to a spike in the ground outside, or to a suitable metal object in the room that goes to an earth. In addition, you should try to keep all mains cables away from sensitive electronic circuits, because they can cause hum if they're too close.

It's worth taking some time to get your recording environment set up properly, because then it'll be easier for you to use at a moment's notice. When the excitement of the purchases wears off, it's surprising how well things need to be set up to prompt you to actually get down to some recording.

2 Studio equipment

Using two cassette players

You really don't *have* to embark upon your money-making exploits armed with anything as elaborate as a four channel multitrack recorder. Initially, a twin cassette deck will do just as well. A similar effect to multitracking can be produced by simply recording your first sound onto one deck, then, whilst dubbing to the second, adding a further track. Alternatively, you could use two separate cassette decks connected up as shown in Figure 2.1.

With such a set-up, you can record a basic track onto the first machine, then switch the second machine to record, replay the first track into it and add a further 'track' live as you do so. This operation can be repeated as many times as you like to build up multi-layered sound pastiches. The only thing that limits the exercise is the gradual loss of audio quality with each successive generation.

Unfortunately, you've got no control over the layered sounds once they're recorded, (with multitrack, they remain separated) and, each time you 'dub', you'll find that the tape hiss increases, and becomes the limiting factor in how many 'tracks' can be constructed in this way. However, all things considered, it is a cheap means of getting into creative recording, and it's how I started — you can buy a four track when the money starts flowing in (more about that later!). Here are a few hints that will assist in maintaining quality when working with conventional cassette machines:

Tape quality
Use the best cassette tape that you can afford. Metal position tapes are best, but if your machine doesn't feature this position then use chrome based ones. I personally favour the TDK SAX.

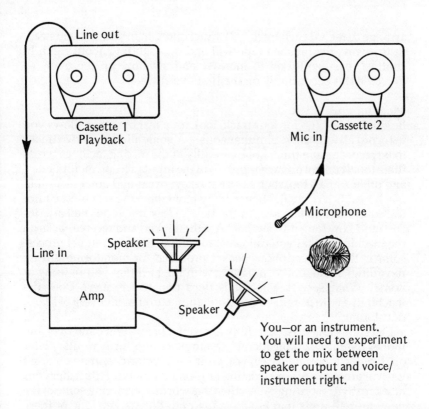

Line out

Cassette 1
Playback

Cassette 2

Mic in

Microphone

Speaker

Line in

Amp

Speaker

You—or an instrument.
You will need to experiment
to get the mix between
speaker output and voice/
instrument right.

Figure 2.1 Dubbing from one tape recorder to another allows you to build up a multi layered track

Recording level
The louder the recorded sounds, the more masked the unwanted background hiss will be. This is known in the recording world as the signal to noise ratio. You should observe this, and record your tracks as loudly as your tape will allow before distortion sets in. Some machines and tapes will allow you to push the levels way up into the red before distorting, leaving the hiss far below — known technically as 'headroom'. Take a close look at the section later in this chapter on meters.

Tone considerations
Treble will diminish on each successive overdub, so, if possible,

arrange to record each track with much more than you feel you need. In this way, the finished tape will end up sounding about right. In contrast, bass will tend to increase and swallow up the track, so decrease this accordingly on the first overdubs.

Meeting multitrack

If you decide to go for four track, look for a machine that allows you to record all four tracks simultaneously — some allow only two tracks to be recorded at a time. Look carefully at the mixing facilities too. Is there tonal control on each input? Will the inputs accept microphones, and other signals too, such as guitars, keyboards and other recording machines? Is it portable? Some of my moneymaking schemes require the equipment to be used 'in the field'. How much do the batteries cost, and how long do they last? Are there 'send and receive' jacks on the machine so that you can use it in conjunction with signal processors? Is there a headphone socket provided for monitoring during recording? Is the unit compatible with the hi-fi that you're using at home? What servicing facilities does the dealer offer? Does the machine have to be returned to the manufacturer in the event of a fault developing?

Questions like these, carefully answered before you hand over any money, could save considerable annoyance and further outlay later on. Finally, if portability isn't on your list of priorities, and you don't wish to press any of your existing hi-fi gear into service to further your new creative recording cause, then it is worth considering some of the new do-it-all units that are creeping onto the market. One of these combines a complete mixer, four track cassette-based recording and playback deck, and a stereo recording deck in one box. And if that isn't enough, it also features a record deck, amplifier, stereo tuner and a pair of speakers, plus a set of four microphones.

Whilst none of these features is likely to be of particularly stunning quality, these machines do their job, and provide you with considerable flexibility for a nominal sum. I feel that they offer a useful stepping stone for home recordists, especially those that don't currently own hi-fi's. If you're unsure about some of the principal facilities on decks and recorders such as these, then the following notes may enlighten you:

Meters

There are two main types of input level meter on today's mixing desks and tape recorders. The first is the VU (volume unit) meter. This is the conventional needle-type unit. On the right hand side of the scale there is a red area, and the way to achieve an optimum recording is to ensure that the meter remains, for the most part, around the start of this section.

The second type of meter is the LED type, made up of a set of lights — the lower ones are usually green or orange, whilst the top ones are red. The aim is to ensure that the top green LED flickers most of the time, with the first red one illuminating only occasionally on the loudest passages. This type of meter reacts much faster to signals fed into it than the VU, making it even easier to set the recorder up accurately.

Inputs
It's best to look for a mixer that has ¼ inch jack sockets for inputs, as most of the devices that you will want to use in conjunction with it, such as microphones and musical instruments, employ this connection. Some mixers are fitted with phono plugs, which will mean that you'll need to buy expensive troublesome adaptors, or make up special signal leads.

Tone controls
Cheaper mixers feature simple bass and treble controls on each individual input channel, whereas more expensive units treat you to something known as equalization. This exists in two forms — parametric and graphic (the latter being dealt with separately later in this chapter). Parametric equalizers feature paired controls: a frequency sweep knob, and an attendant gain knob. There are often several of these pairs operating on each of the mixer's inputs, each handling a specific frequency band. On the most expensive units, there are three, one designed to handle the bass, one for the mid-range, and one for the treble. Using the frequency knob, you can precisely select the exact frequency that you want to process, then, using the gain knob, that specific area of tonal spectrum can be cut or boosted by the required amount. As you can imagine, this provides you with considerably more scope and control than simple bass and treble settings. But do beware — many 'so called' equalizers are nothing more than bass and treble controls in fancy clothing. Look carefully at your chosen desk before you buy. Has it got at least two sets of frequency sweep and gain pairs? If not then it probably won't be a proper equalizer, whatever the salesman insists!

Using a four track recorder

The process of recording on a multitrack is simple. You just record one track at a time, whilst listening to (monitoring) the others. With a four track, you've simply got the facility for recording four sounds — wrong!! You can in fact generate seven good tracks with such a machine. To do this, you mix together the first three tracks that you've recorded, (1, 2 and 3) onto the machine's fourth track. This composite track is known as 'second generation', and is going to be of slightly inferior quality. However, if you are careful to achieve the optimum recording level (see section on meters), then the results will be quite acceptable.

Once you've got your fourth track recorded (we'll call it the rhythm track from now on), plus new material recorded on one and two, you're ready for another bounce (as it is often called). You mix tracks one and two onto track three. This done, you can erase tracks one and two again, and then re-record on them. Let's total up the tracks achieved: First off you recorded three tracks (1, 2 and 3). These were combined on track four. Then you recorded a further two tracks (1 & 2). That makes five tracks. Finally, you recorded two more tracks (1 and 2 again). That totals seven.

It is possible to generate even more tracks by utilizing a master machine. You simply mix down (more details of that later) onto this machine, then bring the completed mix back onto track one of the four track (seven tracks already), and start again. The success of this depends largely on the quality of your mastering machine — and on your patience!

The mixdown

With four completely separate tracks recorded on the machine, the next job is to carefully blend each of these together, and record this blend onto a conventional cassette tape.

Connect the left and right line outputs from the multitrack into the left and right line inputs on a stereo cassette deck. Rewind your tape and, ensuring that each track is switched to playback, listen to your recording. Each track will have its own volume, (and often tone control as well). Adjust each of these to your liking, then put your stereo cassette deck into record and capture the finished product.

Some multitracks have controls labelled 'pan' on them. These are simply balance controls, and allow you to decide where in the stereo image you want each track to occur. These are useful for aircraft sounds, footsteps and suchlike, which can be persuaded to move across from speaker to speaker.

Effects during mixdown

As you know, with mulitrack, you don't have to commit yourself to any effects during the actual recording of the tracks. These can easily be added afterwards. Most machines feature something known as 'send and receive' on each track's output.

It's a simple matter, during mixdown, of connecting the 'send' to the input of an effects unit, (such as reverb, echo, etc) then taking the output of the effects unit into the 'receive' socket. This creates an effects loop. Now, whatever signal is recorded onto that particular track can be treated with the effect. You can experiment with different settings until you come up with something you like, then mix down in the way described above. We'll examine effects in detail shortly.

The ideal set-up
If possible, go for eight track. Secondhand ¼ inch machines, such as the Fostex A8, together with mixers can be bought for around £1000. Don't forget microphones either — I've got a pair of old Audio Technica mics that I use as general purpose mics. Stands for the mics are also essential. The boom type is much more versatile. For a 'silent studio', you'll need a headphone junction box that can be plgged into the headphone socket on your mixer, allowing you to run several pairs of phones simultaneously. However, a monitoring system is also necessary — I simply use a pair of Fostex powered-monitor speakers connected to the mixer, they're great.

Most studios offer some musical equipment too, though this isn't essential. Personally, I think that a good basis for a new studio is a good full-sized key digital synthesizer, an analogue expander (or vice versa), and a sampler, all MIDI linked to a drum machine. As long as the drum machine is digital, then no one's going to complain about the sounds, and with your sampler, you can get any sound you like, whatever the fashion. In addition, the analogue and digital synthesizers balance each other out very well, giving as broad a sound spectrum as anyone could want — I've got a Yamaha DX9 and a Roland JX3P. I can't see a day when I'll need anything else.

It's only worth buying equipment if you're going to derive pleasure and lasting benefit from it, or if it enables you charge more for your services (the latter's the most important in business).

However, the one luxury that you may like to invest in is a sequencer so that you can link all sorts of musical equipment together and make digital tracks. But from a business point of view, think first — will any of you clients want to use such a tool? And if they do, will they be willing to spend several chargeable hours learning how to program it?

It's certain that the home recording market is expanding at a furious pace, and more and more sophisticated equipment is being offered to the consumer. It's easy to get confused and buy things that you don't really need — wasting all your profits. For this reason, I've decided to include a rundown of some of the most common pieces of equipment that you'll encounter at your local home recording dealer. It's better to be well-informed when lots of money's at stake. I'll show you how to make that money later in the book!

Accessories and special effects

These days, there are many little electrical boxes of tricks that can produce superb sounds and process signals in very professional ways. Here are some of them, together with an idea of what they can do. Several manufacturers now produce multi-effects processors, which have all the most useful of these electronic gizmos in one box. They could work out cheaper in the long run.

Digital and analogue delay

These are devices that process a signal by giving it a selectable time delay, so that the output of the line is delayed with respect to the input. The analogue delay line uses a process that is inexpensive enough to offset its less versatile, noisy (i.e. hissy) performance. In contrast, the digital type offers excellent performance but even in guitar pedal form costs around £100.

The amount of delay on the digital machines is adjustable from about one millisecond, (one thousandth of a second) up to 500 milliseconds, or even a full second. This may not sound like much, but it can create a surprising variety of effects such as flanging, chorus and phasing. These three effects sound quite similar, you first heard them on the Small Faces' 'Itchycoo Park' single, if you can remember back that far!

Delay is also excellent for doubling and generally thickening vocal sounds. If you have a weak vocal, put it through a unit set with a fair amount of delay, and you'll sound like two people speaking very tightly together. This is a studio trick known as automatic double tracking, or ADT.

You can also create those long 'dub reggae' echoes with delay units, which can be good fun on your voice, and connected to instrument can sound really weird. Delay's also a fantastic tool when used in conjunction with a drum machine. A very simple drum pattern can take on a whole new dimension when fed through one of these exciting machines.

Even some of the guitar pedal versions of these units are stereo, and so if your system is too, wonderful effects where your vocal or instrument jumps from speaker to speaker can be created at the touch of a button.

Reverberation
Most commonly associated with musical ambience, reverb is a result of a myriad reflected sound waves of an acoustic environment. The character of the reverb depends on the hall. You can experience natural reverb in a large empty room that has a lot of flat reflective surfaces in it, a perfect example is a church. Reverb gives the vicar's voice a powerful commanding quality that makes the congregation listen. Conveniently, this sound is available in a box these days. Once again there are two options, analogue or digital. Analogue machines are usually based on vibrating springs, they're okay for vocals, but if you want to use them on percussive sounds then they tend to overload and go 'boinng'. Digital units, on the other hand, although more expensive, offer the user the chance to simulate all manner of acoustic environments, from a bathroom to St Paul's Cathedral.

Reverb sounds great on almost everything, and can turn a very dead lifeless sound into something that really sparkles with excitement. Almost every modern track that you've ever heard is recorded with reverb. If you could hear the mix without it then you'd realise how important it is.

If you've got a drum machine, then try processing it with reverb, the results are very worthwhile.

Psychoacoustic enhancement
Most of the radio commercials recorded nowadays feature this hard-to-describe processing. In simple terms, it sounds as if the music is about to leap out of the speaker at you. Things are perceived louder and clearer than normal. It's something that you'll have to visit a local music shop to hear in action, but as soon as you have, you'll recognise the benefits.

Equalizers
An equalizer is a device that allows you to make precise tonal adjustments to a signal. You can think of it as a fancy tone control if you like. The term 'equalizer' comes from the concept of using this device to even out, or equalize, overall frequency response, making it flat. Nowadays however, equalization is also used to create powerful bass and shimmering treble in a normally uninteresting signal. If used properly, results can be astounding, but if over-used, the effect becomes noticeable and intrusive on the ear.

The graphic equalizer is made up of a number of slider controls, (filters). The more of these filters that it has, the more precise the tonal adjustments it can make to the audio signal. Some inexpensive types have only four or five filter-sliders, which don't do much more than conventional bass and treble controls. On the other hand, you can get 24 band equalizers, with each slider being spaced one third of an octave apart to cut or boost very specific frequencies within the sound. When choosing a unit, as a guide, the more slider controls that it has on the front panel, then the more useful it's going to be. Sometimes you'll find stereo graphics that have two duplicate sets of sliders. Don't get confused, this doesn't mean that, just because more sliders are in evidence, you'll have more control, and don't let any salesman tell you otherwise.

Compressor
A compressor is a form of amplifier that reduces the dynamic range of a signal. Unlike a normal amp that produces more output when you feed in more input, the compressor produces less as you feed in more. This means that any signal fed into it remains fairly constant in level—loud bits are quietened, and quiet bits made louder. It's very handy when you want to set up levels on a recording then forget about them. It also helps you to produce a punchy sound.

Flanging
There are several well known effects associated with modulation. The first is flanging. It's a combination of delay and low frequency oscillation. It can dramatically thicken the sound of keyboard instruments and produce the 'aircraft type' sound popular among guitarists. Basically, a short delay time is varied with low frequency (LFO) modulation so that the delayed signal moves in relation to the direct signal. These variations in pitch are known as flanging.

Chorus
With the chorus effect, a violin, a keyboard or guitar can sound like an entire ensemble. Chorusing splits the incoming signal into three signals placed at the centre, left and right in the stereo image. Each signal is delayed slightly, and then modulated by LFO. The effect is similar to that of flanging, but not so deep. Cheaper chorus units are mono.

Phasing
Another sound in the same group, and very similar. Phasing lends an animated quality to musical instruments and vocal recordings by

giving them an adjustable pulsing, swirling sound.

Whether or not you decide to 'soup up' your sound with one of these outboard units depends on how fastidious you are, and whether you can be bothered to carry around and wire up extra gear. However, with technology advancing at such a fantastic rate, and equipment that would, just a few years ago, only have been found in top studios, available now at realistic prices, it would be very narrow-minded not to experiment, wouldn't it?

Room tuning

Room tuning is an area where equalization is of use. When you first set up your equipment, you'll normally find that the sound is bright and clear, often to the extent that you decide to increase the bass to compensate. This is because there are a large amount of hard surfaces that reflect high frequencies — and sometimes produce an echo as well — in your empty recording room. Bodies are soft, and absorb these high frequencies, so when you get into your session with a band, suddenly the sound produced from your equipment changes dramatically, from being bright, to being muddy, with matters made worse by the fact that you increased the bass earlier. Even frantic tonal adjustment on the mixer doesn't help very much, (although a mid range boost can be worthwhile in this situation). But if you connect a graphic to the amplifier's input, then you can selectively try cutting or boosting frequencies until a satisfactory monitoring sound is produced.

It's a good idea to have a notebook next to your recorder and write down the settings for your equalizer, and why you've set them the way you have, e.g. compensating for empty room' etc. Over a period of time you'll build up a useful reference book of eq. settings. Then, when a similar situation presents itself again, you can get the optimum sound straight away.

Microphones

Much of the recording that you do to make money will involve the use of microphones. For this reason, it's important to know a little bit about them. This will give you more idea of the best ways to position them relative to the sources that you're recording, and help you to select the best type for your particular applications and budget.

Three types of microphone are commonly used in recording: The dynamic, the condenser and the ribbon. Each works on a different principle. But in each case, it's airwaves hitting a sensitive diaphragm that cause motion inside the mic which is translated into electrical energy. The dynamic type has a coil which moves through a magnetic field. The action of this induces a voltage into the coil, which is then amplified.

The condenser mic is based on a capacitor, and takes advantage of the fact that capacitance changes will show up as voltage changes if the capacitor is biased, or permanently connected to a constant voltage.

The ribbon type of mic uses a thin metal ribbon that catches airwaves. Once upon a time these mics all sounded quite different from one another, but now, with all the gizmos (such as equalizers) that you can use to adjust the tones and so on, you can make them all sound almost identical.

Advantages of different types of mic

The dynamic mic is rugged and simple. The main disadvantage is that it has a lack of response at very low and high frequencies. It also has low output. It's less crisp than a condenser/electret. but resists overload well. Dynamics are good for bass drums and very loud vocalists.

Condenser/electret mics provide good high frequency response compared to dynamics. Trouble is, they need pre-amps to boost their output, and unless these are good, these can add noise and distortion to the signal. Most mics of this type have a battery built into them. The condenser/electret can't take as much input, and is often more prone to overload distortion. Studios use them for acoustic instruments.

Ribbon mics cost a fortune and are very fragile. They've got a great response and give a warm feel to acoustic instruments and voices. Wonderful, but unaffordable as far as we're concerned.

Directionality

Each microphone type can be bought with different pick up character-istics. This decides where you place the microphone in a recording situation. There are three types. The first is the omnidirectional, which means that it captures sound equally from all directions. The second is the bidirectional, which picks up sound mainly from the front and back, but not the sides. The third type is the unidirectional, or cardoid. These pick up sound mainly from in front of the microphones. With each, you'll find that low frequencies are less directional than high frequencies.

Microphone directionality

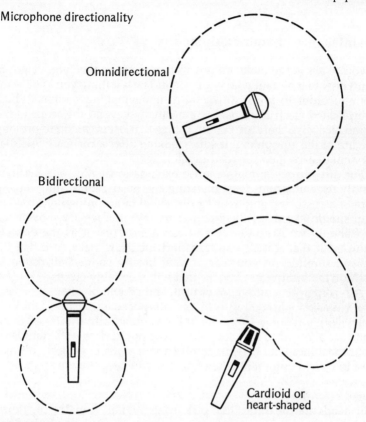

Figure 2.2 The three different types of microphone and their directionality diagrams

Microphone squeal

Known technically as *feedback*, this is caused by the microphone picking up the speaker output. If it becomes too high, the circuit oscillates and the output becomes independent of the input, causing the unpleasant noise. Remove the offending frequency and you've cured the problem. This is where a graphic equalizer is useful once again, but only if it has sufficient filter-sliders. I use one made by Tandy. It's a ten band device, and allows me to alleviate feedback problems without adversely affecting the sound. Whilst a five band unit may cure the squeal, in doing so, it changes a bigger chunk of the sound, rendering the 'cure' useless — unless you want your system to resemble a transistor radio, that is.

25

Maintenance of your equipment

If you're aiming to make money from recording, then you've got to learn how to maintain your equipment. The last thing you want is for your recorder to break down on a moneymaking session. Whilst complicated electrical repairs are normally beyond the scope of the home recordist, there are certain things that users can do to prolong the life of the equipment. It's like looking after a car really: regular servicing keeps it on the road much longer.

For our purposes, maintenance extends to treating the machine kindly, cleaning and demagnetizing the heads, lubricating, taking care of accessories, and treating the actual tapes properly.

You shouldn't subject the recorder to any unnecessary movement, and should set it up gently and carefully. Treat it as the delicate equipment that it is. If you transport the gear, make sure that it's stowed carefully in your car or van, ideally padded all round to cushion the bumps and knocks that will inevitably occur.

A recorder generates a lot of heat, and should be given the maximum assistance in cooling — that means not covering any of the vent holes with anything. Component life is drastically shortened if circuits are allowed to run hot. Don't ever put glasses with liquids on your machines, and be very careful about spills in general. It's also best to cover equipment when not in use to keep the dust out.

Head cleaning

The heads are the things that pick up the signals from the recording tape on your machine. Yards of tape scrapes past them all the time, and consequently, they soon begin to get dirty. To maintain the sound quality of your tape deck, they need occasional cleaning. You can do this by using a soft cotton bud, swabbed in head cleaning fluid, available cheaply from most dealers. Keep cleaning until there is no brownish residue left on the head.

After the heads, clean the capstan and pinch roller — this is the rubber ring and metal post that the tape passes between. It's visible on the right hand side of your deck, next to the head cover. Don't clean the rubber bit with the head cleaning fluid, as this can sometimes make it crack. Instead, use a little warm water. It's good practice to clean these parts at the end of every recording session.

Demagnetizing

Iron and steel, which is used for most of the tape transport machinery, is very sensitive to magnetism. This can degrade the recorded signal by erasing high frequencies and causing unwanted hiss. You can't entirely eliminate stray magnetism, but you can substantially reduce it to an acceptable level. To do this you need a device called a demagnetizer. These are available from most specialist hi-fi shops. They might even let you borrow one. Once you've got access to the demagnetizer, the procedure is as follows:

1 Turn the tape recorder off and get all tapes well out of the way.
2 Plug in the demagnetizer, holding it at least 24 inches away from the tape heads or any tapes
3 Move the tip of the demagnetizer towards the tape head, coming as close as possible *without* actually touching it.
4 Wave the tip from side to side across the face of the head, then slowly withdraw the tip from the head.
5 Turn off the demagnetizer while it's at least 24 inches away from the tape deck or any tapes.

It's the slow withdrawal of the probe that accomplishes the actual process of demagnetism.

Tape care

Once you get underway, your tapes will become very important to your business. They will have material on them that is worth a lot of money to you. It's essential, therefore, that they're treated properly. Any electrical device, if placed close to a tape, can partially erase it. For this reason, you should keep your tapes well away from speakers, mains leads, soldering irons, transformers, headphones and TV sets — to name but a few.

Tapes should be stored in a cool dry place, avoiding moisture. They should also be kept out of strong sunlight. Keep your fingers off the surface of the tape too — greasy finger marks will lead to dropouts in the sound as that part of the tape passes the heads.

3 Moneymaking ideas

Each of the following ideas *will* make you money. All you need is dedication and the determination to back them up. Many of them can be started with the minimum of recording equipment. The money that you make from these ideas will allow you to buy more sophisticated gear as you go along. Pick a scheme and start *now*!!

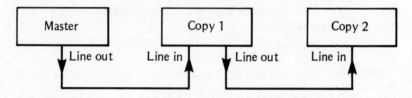

Figure 3.1 Daisy chaining recorders for more efficient duplicating

Cassette copying

I'm convinced that you could set up a service of this kind almost anywhere in the country and make money! There's always going to be a local entertainer, band or drama group who need duplicates of their material, and if you play your cards right, you could end up by recording their masters as well as copying them (another idea?) Let's look at the two different types of copying service available:

Real time and high speed
In real time copying, both the master, and the slave recorders run at normal speed. For cassettes, this is $1^7/_8$ inches per second. So, one C60 cassette is going to take a whole hour to copy. On the face of it, this is a ridiculous state of affairs, because if your client puts in an order for 40 tapes, then you're going to have a whole week's work ahead of you. So, how can you minimize copying time? — easy! The answer is to

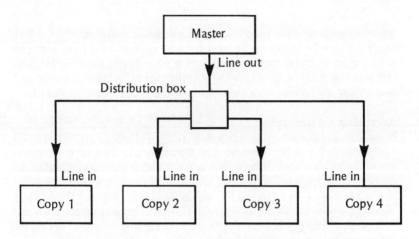

Figure 3.2 A distribution box helps to improve the quality of the duplicated recording

daisy-chain several cassette recorders together, as shown in Figure 3.1.

The cassettes don't copy any quicker, but you can do more than one at a time. In the interests of quality, you may find it better (especially if you're chaining a lot of machines together), to run them from a distribution box, as shown in Figure 3.2.

This real time system is probably the best approach to begin with, because you can easily expand the system as the work begins to flow in. From a marketing point of view, it's also better to mention 'real time' in your ad, because many people still think (mistakenly), that it's an infinitely better system than high speed duplication.

This high speed copying is your other option. It can yield much better results than real time, but to get these results, you'd have to spend a lot of money. My own copier is an Otari DP 4040 C2, which costs around £3000. It copies two cassettes at a time, at eight times the normal speed. Although fast and convenient, with results that are second to none, you need to copy a heck of a lot of tapes to recoup that investment and make a profit!

Your decision

I suggest that you begin your venture using real time copying, with one master cassette deck, and two identical slaves. Try to make sure that all three machines are the same make and model. Apart from the fact that a dealer may give you a discount if you buy all three, all the recordings should then sound the same. It would be foolish to recommend a specific machine, as there are so many on the market that are virtually the same. Hopefully, you may already have some in your studio that you can use. When you've got your machines sorted out, wire them up, taking care to keep the signal and mains leads well away from each other to avoid hums and buzzes (see Chapter 2).

Accepting master tapes

Believe me, client's master tapes will come in all shapes, sizes, speeds and formats if you let them, so don't! For simplicity's sake, I recommend that you accept only high quality cassette masters recorded on chrome or metal tape. It may seem an odd thing to say, but honestly, you'll have all sorts of problems and unnecessary hassles if you start messing around with a multitude of different master tapes. Remember, you're doing this to make money. Offer a reel-to-reel service if you must, but charge extra for it!

Your most important single item is the cassette itself. If your tapes jam up, shed tons of oxide and so on, then your customers are going to lose confidence in you — fast, and you're going to have to replace any 'faulties' out of your profits to keep them pacified.

I've researched cassettes very carefully. The most common problem appears to be that of shells as opposed to tape. If they haven't been manufactured to the high tolerance required, then you're on dodgy ground to start with, and you're going to get problems both with jamming, and azimuth. It's worth getting it right first time, even if it costs you a few pence more. Buy shells with five screws holding them together, as this is usually a sign of better manufacture. before finally choosing a supplier, ask to be sent some random samples and put them through the mill before committing yourself to a batch.

Now, on to the tape itself. I personally only ever use three different types — Agfa Magnetite 12 is a high quality ferric tape which has quite outstanding high frequency recording level. You should expect to pay about 60p for a C60. Professional sources inform me that 'print through' has been experienced with this tape, but I can't say that I've ever noticed it. BASF LHD is another good reliable IEC 1 bias tape with very low drop out. Expect to pay around 50p for a C60. Finally, Zonal Max 3 is my personal favourite. It tends to give a somewhat brighter recording and, as such, compensates for any slight treble loss occurring in the copying process. I'd advise you to obtain samples of each tape, and draw your own conclusions. Don't forget that you'll also have to budget for a library case (about 7p), and for printing.

Printing

If you decide to offer a printing service, then you're going to be faced with two different requirements — the side labels for the cassettes, and the inlay cards for the cases. My advice is to initially just cater for the side labels. That way, you can ensure that your phone number appears securely stuck to each cassette, giving you free advertising and the chance of repeat business. Normally, your cassette supplier will be able to handle all of the printing from his end. You simply supply double sized camera-ready artwork. He will stick the labels onto the cassettes for you before sending them. It's best to allow about £50 for 2000 labels initially, although subsequent print runs will be cheaper because there will be no origination costs to contend with.

A tip about inlay cards — if you're going to offer this service, then either do your own, or get an arty friend to produce the artwork, and use rub-on type lettering (Letraset) to augment it. Duplicate the finished work, and arrange for four inlay cards to fit onto a piece of A4 paper. Present this to a local printer, and be prepared to cut up the finished work yourself. You might expect to pay £5 per 100 sheets of A4 — that's 400 inlay cards. One other tip — don't get involved in printing two or more colours. The price suddenly soars. Use one colour of ink on a contrasting colour card, it looks just as good!

Your prices
I suggest that the larger the order, then the cheaper the unit price per copy. I don't think that it's good practice to hold any cassettes in stock. It's far better to open an account with a good supplier, then you can simply pick up the phone, and get your order sent within a day or two. Working this way, you can ensure that you only use the correct tape lengths required, thus avoiding wastage. Here's a suggested price list:

Quantity	Length	Unit price
25-49	C30	92p
	C60	133p
50-100	C30	83p
	C60	119p

It's best to avoid handling any orders larger than 100 in the early days. Quite honestly, on a local level, you probably won't get bigger orders anyway. These prices are only given as guidance, but are currently realistic for BASF LHD. They don't include any postage, printing or library cases though! Try to find out what prices any other copying facilities in your area are charging, and compete favourably.

Advertising

Initially, my advice is to stay local. You'll have less competition for your services, and usually no postage charges for batches of cassettes sent to clients. It's also unlikely that you'll be required to handle long runs that you'd struggle on anyway. After a few months, try venturing outside your area and go for some national advertising in the music and drama magazines. But remember to allow for postage and packing in your prices.

Start your advertising in a local newspaper — I've found that the best days are Thursdays and Fridays. Place the ad in the classified section under the musical heading and expect to pay around £12 for two insertions. Experience has shown that you need to keep the advert in the publication, week in, week out to get good results, so build up advertising into your prices too.

As far as the advert itself goes, there are certain key words that have instant appeal. They are Free! Special! New! How to! You can! and Now! Work as many of them as you into your copy for maximum response:

NEW CASSETTE COPYING SERVICE
SPECIAL RATES AND FREE QUOTATIONS

You can find reputable cassette suppliers in most of the national music papers, such as *NME*, *Melody Maker*, and *Sounds*.

Get the message

Answerphones, or, to give them their correct title, telephone answering machines, are becoming increasingly popular, not only in the commercial environment, but also in the home. We've all put the receiver down on one of the nasty things at one time or the other, but why? I think that, in most cases, it's the dreary commentary at the other end of the line that puts us off. Perhaps if the message was more interesting, and fun to listen to, then the caller would actually get as far as leaving a message. So let's look at some ways in which you can make some money out of this state of affairs, and set-up your own answerphone message recording service.

If you've got a basic four track recording system and a smattering of musical ability, then you're halfway there already. Your messages don't have to include any genuine musical content, but if you have got the ability to produce simple twenty second snippets, then you can make your service even more appealing to potential clients. You're going to be faced with two different types of customer: business, where you'll hope to make most money, and private users. Let's look at each type in turn

Business users
In most circumstances, businesses are fairly serious establishments. You must ensure that your customized message dovetails into their commercial outlook properly. For example, a lawyer won't want the same treatment as a singing telegram agency. I think that each business client's message should be recorded as an individual project, as opposed to the off-the-shelf approach that we're going to adopt for private subscribers. The message and the optional musical backdrop should precisely fit your client's needs within his business world. To begin with, I would advise you to supply any business clients that you manage to procure, with a form similar to that set out below.

Client's name...
Client's address..
Message required ....
Musical content yes/no ....
Voice male/female ....

Make sure you obtain a 25% deposit, so that at least you will have covered some of your time, should the client back out. We'll discuss the actual recording process later on.

Private customers
Private subscribers are an altogether different affair. They don't actually rely on their answerphone to make them money, so you are not going to be able to charge them as much for your services. Most domestic answerphones are regarded as more of a novelty than their commercial counterparts, and are aimed more at offering friends and relations a chance to leave simple messages, often in fun more than anything else. Most users would welcome some amusing message which would undoubtedly be destined to become the talk of the family.

To achieve sales in this market sector, you will have to offer low prices and hope for a large number of sales — the opposite in fact to the sales pitch in the business world. It would not be viable to produce individually customized messages for every client, and so what you should do is record a library of good non-specific (i.e. not mentioning the client's name and number) messages. Hence the term 'off-the-shelf'. Here's an idea to start you off:

"Hello this is the butler speaking. I'm sorry, but my employers are away at present. However, if you wish to leave a message with me, then I shall ensure that they receive it on their return".

Incidentally, messages should be no more than about eighteen seconds in duration. To make the best of your messages, you need a good versatile voice. If yours doesn't fit the bill, then contact a local amateur drama group — there's always one nearby.

Recording
Firstly, record the vocal message on to track 1 of the multitrack. Having done this, swap tapes and produce three 20 second pieces of background music reflecting different moods. Mix the music, and master it onto a separate machine in mono. Dub these three different pieces back on to the tape on which you recorded the vocal. Arrange for them to appear simultaneously on tracks two three, and four, to coincide with the message.

Now all you need to do is fade up the required musical background to your client's requirements without any further work on your part. Bear in mind however, that most answerphone messages are twenty seconds long. If you make any production shorter than this, then there will be a pregnant pause before the 'talk now' bleep. Any longer will mean a loss of the end of the message.

Formats
There are several different types of tapes used in answerphones, but by far the most common is the 20 second duration, endless loop, standard size cassette. These are available from Tandy stores countrywide. They're fitted with a metal stop-foil to ensure that messages begin and end correctly. This stop-foil won't be operational on your studio deck, and so when you are mixing down onto these cassettes, you must ensure that you start recording directly after the foil, pressing stop promptly after 20 seconds, otherwise you'll rub off the message that you've just recorded.

If your client has a non-standard type of answerphone tape such as the little dictating machine tapes, then things are going to get a bit more difficult for you. You should insist that he supplies the blank tape, as you may have trouble obtaining one of the correct format. You're obviously not going to be able to dub the finished message onto your studio cassette in the normal way. Consequently, your client will have to suffer the inconvenience of bringing his answerphone machine to your studio. Set it up in its message-record mode, run your message from the multitrack, and capture it on his machine, using its built-in mic. Not a terribly professional state of affairs, but one that does in fact work surprisingly well. It has even been known to yield better results than doing things the conventional way. This is because the dynamic range is compatible with the similarly limited range of the receiver.

Prices

I suggest for the off-the-shelf, non-specific messages that we've discussed, you should charge £7.99 for speech only and £9.99 for speech and music (choice of three backgrounds).

If you followed my advice for recording the music, then you're getting an extra £2 each time, for simply pushing up the fader on track 2, 3 or 4, offering your client a choice of three different musical mood backgrounds. As I said earlier, the commercial world is where the money lies. A business relies on the telephone to get most of its work. Every time someone hangs up on hearing an answerphone, then it's lost money, possibly thousands of pounds! If you can minimize these lost opportunities, then you're in with a chance of selling your services, and that should be your main sales-pitch to prospective business clients. You can use the same musical backgrounds that you've already produced, but you need to be prepared to produce individual customized messages for every different client. This means more work on your part, but it will be worth it. Rates that I recommend you seek for customized answerphone messages are: speech only £25, speech and music £40.

To make this a worthwhile package, you must ensure that your production is professionally produced with the vocal delivery tailor made to fit the company image. Remember, if your clients can do it themselves, then they will. Make your message special and provide some demos for potential customers to hear before they book.

Marketing

So how do you market your service? Well, first of all, you get out your *Yellow Pages* and let your fingers do the walking, whilst your pen jots down the name and address of every company that states 'twenty-four-hour' in their advertisement. Then send a letter, enclosing an sae to all of them. Here's a rough draft for you:

Dear ...
As a user of a telephone answering machine, you must doubtless be aware that a considerable volume of business is lost through potential clients ringing off directly your message begins. This results in hundreds, or perhaps thousands, of pounds worth of potential business going astray

I am able to minimize this loss for you. I specialize in production of effective answerphone messages, designed specifically around your precise requirements. Contact me now before you lose any more of you valuable business. You'll be glad you did!

Yours ...

To obtain private customers, then you should advertise in the personal section of the local (or if you can afford it, national) press. It's also worth contacting shops that sell answerphones, and offering them your library on a sale-or-return basis. You may even like to try for a feature in your local paper. They should be interested in new ideas (see Chapter 5).

Location recording

Are you willing to transport your recording equipment around? Do you fancy recording bands but lack the necessary space at home? If so, then location recording could be for you!

There are two ways in which a group of musicians can improve. The first is practice — lots of it. The second is by hearing what they sound like to others. This hearing process allows faults to be rectified before anyone else's eardrums suffer. Many bands don't possess recording equipment with which to record their rehearsals, and the few that do own suitable machines can't be bothered to set them up each time a practice session commences, let alone keep an eye on levels and suchlike. The home recordist has both the equipment, and the expertise.

At the same time, there are a great many bands who have made the jump from the garage or rehearsal room to the stage (but only just). Those early performances are critical to their development. Problems must be ironed out, and fast — landlords have ears too! The situation almost begs you to step in and offer you recording services. A good quality recording of these early performances could act as essential reference material for the fledgling band.

Additionally, in almost any area, there are experienced bands too. They've practised hard, and are past the self-criticizing stage. They perform regularly and make good money. Over a period of time, they've gained a loyal following in their locality. They need you too. Recording one of their live performances and releasing it on cassette to their fans allows both you and the band to make some money. You can record the performance and produce the copies (as we've already seen). Let's examine ways to satisfy this demand.

Live recording
For this, only the barest minimum of equipment is necessary. A good quality two-track and a couple of microphones will be more than adequate to start with. As you make money, you can add more equipment. But there are two initial steps to be taken. Firstly, persuade the band that your services are indispensable and secondly offer a realistic price.

In a live situation, your band (and I'm thinking here about the novice ones) will want the best recording that they can get for posterity, as much as reference. To them, the music business is an exciting new world.

If you own a portable multitracker, then you can offer quite outstanding facilities. Arrange for the live recording to be a stereo spread over tracks one and two. This can be recorded with microphones on stands at either side of the stage, or directly from the mixing desk if everything's miked up. However, it's worth ensuring that mics are not placed to close to the PA speakers, or anything not miked up will be inaudible. Mic stands placed on the stage will pick up vibrations from the band moving about which will ruin the recording. If on-stage placement is unavoidable, then remove the mics from their stands, and cushion them in soft sponge on the floor, or suspend them from the ceiling on wires.

The price that you charge should depend on two key points. The first is how long you'll be in attendance, and the second is how much travelling there is involved. To calculate travelling expenses, draw concentric circles on a map. Your home base should act as the centre, and each subsequent circle should represent a different higher price band. Using a system such as this makes it easy to immediately quote travelling expenses for every local destination. The figures within your price bands will obviously depend on what sort of transport you're using.

Once the performance has been safely captured on tape, you can offer the band the chance to polish it up. If you're using a multitrack, then two tracks are spare. Perhaps the singer would like to double-track his vocal. Maybe the lead guitarist wants to add some extra twiddly bits. Wouldn't that snare drum sound better supported by a Simmons sound? Post-production work such as this could probably be done back at your home base, and charged for accordingly. How about this for a rate card?

ATTENDANCE AT CONCERT FOR A MAXIMUM OF FOUR HOURS CULMINAT-
ING IN THE PRODUCTION OF A STEREO RECORDING OF THE SHOW. TO
INCLUDE ONE CASSETTE COPY — £15
POST PRODUCTION WORK — £5 PER HOUR
FURTHER CASSETTE COPIES BY ARRANGEMENT

If the band are experienced and have their own 'rentacrowd', then you
should push your cassette copying service hard. My advice is to offer
package prices of say 25, 50 or 100 copies including inlay cards.

The one final thing that you should bear in mind is that work of this
nature is always done in *one take*. You must get that recording to sound
respectable first time if you want to maintain your credibility and get
paid!

Rehearsal recording

In my experience, practice sessions seem to last for a maximum of
about four hours. With this in mind, I suggest that you charge £8 plus
travelling. If the session lasts longer than this, then you should charge
£3 per extra hour (or part hour). These rates are fairly low because the
band are going to be paying you out of their own pockets, and they
haven't begun performing yet. Nevertheless, this is balanced out by
the fact that they could be a useful source of regular work for you if
they practice often. Also, given that most bands split up, you could
soon find yourself with four clients instead of one — all in separate
bands — great for you!

Your most difficult job won't be the recording itself, it'll be actually
persuading the band to use you. You must look at things from their
points of view. They'll be paying you money for something that they
could do themselves with a stereo cassette (could, but probably can't
be bothered). Tell them that after each song, you'll have an instant
playback ready to run, so that they can evaluate their progress.
Include a free cassette copy of the session for the band to take away.

Offer to assist them in learning difficult phrases. For example, if the
lead guitarist is struggling with his solo, and the rest of the band are
losing their patience, ask them to play the backing track without the
lead solo, and record it. Now send them away for a break. Play the
track back and get the lead guitarist to play along. You can re-run the
piece as many times as you like, because tape recorders don't lose their
patience — ever!

However much you aspire to be a great producer, don't get involved in playing discussions. You may yearn for the perfect recording, but the band won't. Avoid spending long periods of time posi-
tioning microphones and setting levels. Just concentrate on getting a

basic record of what's being played down on tape. Be unobtrusive and efficient.

I don't suggest that you set-up more than two microphones for this job, as it won't make you any extra money for your trouble. Also, you'd end up hindering the band as you struggle to mix levels correctly. They've got enough to worry about already, without you asking them to run through some songs half a dozen times.

Location and practice recording need not be confined to bands. Any audio-based project will benefit from this treatment.

Advertising

Beware of spending too much on advertising. I suggest, in this particular instance, that you try a postcard campaign. Most music shops and many record shops have in-store noticeboards. A well-worded postcard placed on these boards will cost only a few pence per week, and can be extremely effective. You may also like to consider expanding your campaign to include post office and newsagents too.

It's important to monitor any advertising campaign very carefully. Keep notes of each advertisement placed, along with how much it costs. Underneath this, mark the number of enquiries that it has generated and orders received. Any adverts that don't yield any response should be discontinued. But give each a chance, and retain the advert for a couple of months before deciding to stop it. You'll often find that people need to see it several times before being stimulated into any positive action. Here's an idea for your postcard:

LOCATION RECORDING
FROM REHEARSALS TO LIVE CONCERTS
YOUR PERFORMANCE CAPTURED IN FULL STEREO
MULTITRACK OVERDUBBING
EXPERIENCED OPERATOR
VERY ATTRACTIVE RATES FOR BANDS
TEL. 123456 NOW!

Listen and learn

If you are a musician, I wonder if you have ever thought of turning your skills towards teaching others? Maybe not. Perhaps it's a lack of confidence, space, or both. Or is it that you simply don't have the patience? Well, here's an easy way to draw pupils from the whole country, as opposed to just your immediate area, without any hassle. In fact, without even seeing any of them at all. What's the secret...?

Tuition tapes.

In recent years there has been a growing interest in teaching cassettes, and people have realized that they can, in fact, be extremely effective. This can work to your advantage. Let's examine some money-making schemes.

The four most common instruments in rock are guitar, bass, drums and keyboards. I'll take guitar as an example first. Before you begin, you must remember that a teaching tape *must* teach. Cassettes of this type sell in large quantities because they offer novel ways of presenting boring information. Most purchasers have a rudimentary knowledge of their chosen instrument already, and are on the look out for short-cuts to improve. From the guitarist's point of view, this is usually in the direction of improvised lead work. In the past, guitarists simply twiddled around with lead scales unaware of how they integrated with other instruments.

You can change all that with your teaching tapes. To gain maximum improvement in the minimum time the student can be offered a backing track to play along with. It is beyond the scope of this book to actually show you how to teach a musical instrument (you could buy *my* tapes instead). What I aim to do is concentrate on helping you to present *your* pearls of wisdom, and make you richer for doing it. So, let's talk about the recording itself.

I suggest that you produce a simple backing track on your multi-track machine, and use whatever instrumentation that you happen to have available/can play. Ensure that, whatever you record, you keep one track spare. On this you should record a demonstration improvised lead part. This done, mix the backing in mono to appear equally in both speakers. Now, pan the lead track hard to one side of the mix. This is shown in Figure 3.3

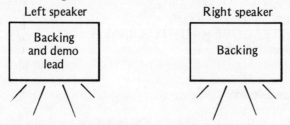

Figure 3.3 Mixing the tracks as shown helps the student musician learn the part

Using this novel way of mixing, the student can, assuming that they have a stereo player, turn the balance control to the extreme left and play along with the backing plus lead out of the left speaker. Alternatively, by simply sliding the balance control to the right he can listen to the backing on its own, and play along without guidance. As the student gets more confident he can gradually reduce the sound of the left speaker, thus reducing the guide track until he is playing along on his own with the backing. To my knowledge, there are no tapes on the market that utilize such a technique, although I've got a feeling that there will be soon!

The same principle can be applied to bass, drums, keyboards and vocal instruction tapes. For example, for drummers you could record the complete backing track and mix the drums into one speaker, in similar fashion to the demonstration lead mention earlier. Figure 3.4 shows what I mean:

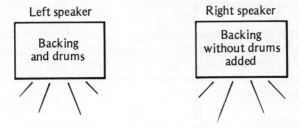

Figure 3.4 Tuition tape format for drummers

Whilst I fully appreciate that perhaps you can't play all the instruments yourself, I'd wager that you have some musical friends. With a little thought you could soon be tapping their talents, together with your own, to form a profitable little business. If you have trouble persuading them, then you could point out that playing a few tracks in your studio, and getting paid for it, is much more appealing than tortuous trips in a freezing transit van to distant venues, often for less reward.

Finally on the subject, you should remember to budget for some photocopying. You need to produce a simple inlay card, and also some guidance notes for users of your tapes. These should include any scales etc. in diagram form. Make everything as big and as simple as possible. 99.9% of all potential rock musicians are put off by boring musical theory.

Backing track tapes
At my Sound Workshop, I've produced a series of 'Rocktrax' tapes that have, over the last five years, sold exceptionally well. The concept is simple but seems to have proved extremely useful to musicians of all standards. I record a series of backing tracks in a variety of different

styles, ensuring that each instrument used has a track to itself. The tracks are then mastered four times, leaving out a different instrument each time. So, on tapes destined for bassists, the bass part is left out of the mix. This offers the bass student an 'instant band' to play in. The cassette is played back at home on the hi-fi, and 'jammed along' to. It's much more fun than isolated practising. It improves timing and allows the player to gauge personal progress effectively.

Working in this way, I produced four different products from one recording session (guitar, bass, drums and keyboard mixes). To give the players some guidance in what to play, I left their instrument in the mix for the first couple of bars. To go with the tape I typed a simple information sheet giving details of the key the piece was in, what style it was, and the format. For example:

KEY OF G: BLUES: 12 BAR FORMAT (G, C, D)

Together with this, I made up a simple inlay card, which was printed in one colour by a local printer. I duplicated the cassette myself (in the way we've discussed at the start of the chapter) and offered them at £5 each. To date, I've sold over 300. Perhaps I shouldn't have let you in on the secret.

Sales outlets

You may be able to put pressure on your local music shop to sell your tapes for you, especially if you've bought all of your recording equipment from them. After all, the chances are that any money you make from the project will probably soon find its way back into their till voluntarily anyway. To encourage more sales, I offered a discount system whereby if someone bought the whole set, I would knock of 20%. Also, in each cassette I inserted a photocopy. This acted as a discount voucher for subsequent volumes. The customers kept the top half which entitled them to a £1 discount from the next volume. To qualify, they had to tear off the bottom section, fill in their name and address stating when and where bought, and send it to me. This enabled me to build up a list of people who liked the tapes, and were in the market for further copies. It also allowed me to decide whether or not it was worth producing further volumes. It was — and for a ready made market.

If you've got your act together in the cassette copying department and are confident that you are able to meet demand then you should consider an advert in the national music press.

Other opportunities

You don't have to limit your instructional cassettes to music, how about language training? There really is tremendous scope in this field, but unfortunately, tremendous competition to match. You can however, sidestep that and avoid the marketing headaches that are associated with it. The best plan is to contact the language department heads of local colleges and universities. Outline your idea, and make it known that you have the recording facilities available to handle such a task. Many of them would welcome audio supplements for their courses, and would happily send a tutor to your studio to handle the content — all you need do is make the recording, the copies, and negotiate a fee.

It has been proved beyond doubt that the audio medium has more impact than the written word. A friend of mine who is the marketing director of a large company tells me that he often distributes 'Motivation tapes' to his sales force, with quite startling results. They can be played in the car by the reps on their way to appointments. They are designed to produce a confident attitude, and remind the salesman of the correct sales approach. The tapes apparently work exceptionally well, and have a positive effect on sales. The only trouble is, the recording quality is dodgy, and they would like to make the tapes more interesting to listen to, using music and sound effects. I haven't got the contract to produce these yet, but I'm trying.

There's no reason why you shouldn't produce such mini-epics. How about sending a mail-shot to the double glazing companies in your area? They are always in stiff competition with each other and anything to improve sales will be given serious considerations — at a price. *Try it.*

A record of the event

Have you ever fancied having your recordings transferred to disc but been unable to afford the pressing charges? This idea offers you the opportunity without spending a penny. In fact, you *make* money out of the deal.

There has always been an interest in preserving some record of special occasions. Money in these situations seems to flow like water — ask any wedding photographer. Recently, video has made inroads into this particular market. Initially, it may appear that there's no call for sound-only recordings. However, nothing could be further from the truth.

When offering your recording services for a special occasion, there are several things to bear in mind. Firstly, the service offered must be different or better than your clients are able to produce themselves. Secondly, you won't get opportunities for a second take — it has to be right first time.

Anyone can, if they have the inclination, record a ceremony such as a wedding, reasonably well, armed with no more than a simple cassette recorder and a microphone. The results will be far from stunning, but often acceptable to the happy couple and the immediate family with nothing to compare.

With your recording equipment, you could, on the other hand, produce that stunning recording. But even that is not enough to justify your fee. You need something much more unique. How about offering the finished stereo product on LP record?

The occasions

Remember that you're working in sound alone, and a lot of events, such as birthday parties and anniversaries, which are the staple diet of videographers and photographers, are non-starters for you. You need to aim for ceremonies where something important is being said, sung or both. The obvious ones are weddings and christenings, although even the latter is more of a visual one. In fact, most of the best sound only events occur in churches.

A word of warning — don't accept bookings until the project has been discussed with the vicar concerned. Make an appointment to go and see him and impress upon him that you will remain very unobtrusive throughout the proceedings. A donation to the church fund often works very well!

For extra money, you could offer to attend the reception to record the speeches. I suggest that your price list states two prices — one for attendance at the church only, and one to include a visit to the reception. It's advisable to set a time limit on the length of time you will be in attendance. I can remember having to sit for 2½ hours, watching everyone eating their meal before the speeches took place. I was starving hungry, bored out of my skull, and on the verge of begging for morsels by the time the speeches began.

The recording

Once inside the church, act professionally and unobtrusively. Stay well out of the way of the guests. I remember an irate mother telephoning me the day after a wedding, complaining that I hadn't turned up. I had, and had made a very good recording too! I don't think she really believed me until the finished disc was in her hand.

Arrive to set up a couple of hours before the event. It would be extremely useful to have an assistant to help you, especially in setting microphone levels. The equipment used depends largely upon what you've got available. Ideally, a multitrack machine should be used.

Four tracks and four microphones is the ideal set-up. These mics are best positioned according to the layout given in Figure 3.5.

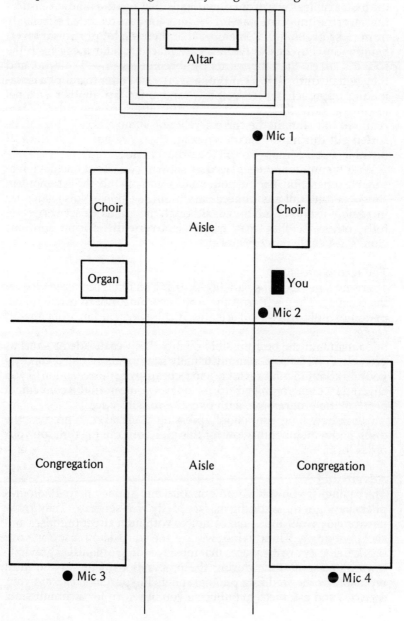

Figure 3.5 Recommended mic locations for recording a wedding ceremony in church   45

Extension mic and mains cables will probably be required. If at all possible, balanced mic lines should be used. However, at least keep the mains cables away from signal leads. Setting up as shown ensures that all of the important parts of the ceremony are recorded effectively from close proximity. Remember that there's a lot of natural reverberation in churches, If the mics are placed too far away from the sound sources, then the words can become swamped in echo, and they will be difficult to hear properly. It's far better to adopt a close-miking approach where possible, and open up another channel feeding a more distant microphone to introduce any extra reverb required to maintain the correct 'religious atmosphere'. This can be sorted out during the mixdown stage if you've got a four track. If possible, use a compressor on the principal mic.

With the microphones placed as shown, you should achieve reasonable separation. Back at your studio, you can mix the ceremony in stereo, editing out any unnecessary boring sections. Noise gates are incredibly useful in mixdown, although they must be set very carefully, otherwise they may trigger inadvertently during spurious clunks as people move chairs etc.

The record pressing
There are a number of small disc-pressing facilities scattered all over the country. They will transfer your recording, not to conventional pressings, but to direct-cut acetates. In this way you can order one-off copies.

To maintain the best possible quality, keep each side as short as possible. A wedding ceremony usually lasts for about half an hour. If you add about 15 minutes for the speeches during the reception (if you covered it) then you'll end up, as long as you can find a convenient break in the programme, with two 22½ minute sides

Check how long your chosen pressing plant takes to produce the discs, and remember to allow for this plus your mixing time, on your order form.

Advertising
The saying 'If you can't beat 'em, join 'em!'applies here. Photographers have got the wedding market pretty well sewn up. They know it extremely well, and come complete with high street premises and shop windows! These windows are the ideal showcase for your service, as they are the places that most wedding organisers gravitate towards at some time during the preparations. Contact the most reputable of the wedding photographers in your area, explain your services, and ask them to publicize you in return for a commission.

Get some business cards printed, together with a poster. Mine read

YOUR SPECIAL OCCASION CAPTURED ON RECORD
THE IDEAL WEDDING ALBUM
A BIG HIT WITH THE FAMILY!

I persuaded a top local photographer to lend me a corner of his window display, and suspended two of these posters from it, on threads, together a couple of LPs with the labels blanked out. On these blanks I wrote (using rub-on lettering) 'Your Wedding'. It was so unique that it drew quite a lot of interest, and consequently I was visiting churches that summer on a much more regular basis than I ever had before — and getting paid for it!

Prices
Unless another home recordist nearby has read this book and decided to set up in your area, then you'll be offering a unique service without competition, and so you can, within reason, pitch your prices wherever you wish. First of all though, you need to find out exactly how much the direct cut acetates will cost, as this will be your principal outlay. In my experience, this is normally between £20 and £25 per 12 inch disc. With this in mind, I would envisage charging around £60 plus travelling expenses, adding a further £15 to the price if you are required to cover the speeches too. Further discs can then be offered to members of the family for £35 each.

If you find that prospective clients are put off by these prices, then you could offer a 7 inch single which just includes edited highlights of the service. You'll still make the same profit, because the reduction will be in the pressing. Finally, remember to insist on a 50% non-refundable deposit to cover your time, and/or the cost of pressing in the event that they back out.

Tell us another one...

Even if you can't sing and your dog clears off when you pick up a musical instrument, there's still a chance that you can make money from this idea. All you need is a good imagination, a reasonable speaking voice and a tape recorder — even a standard stereo cassette will do for a start. Although, as we shall see, a multitrack and a few pieces of outboard equipment can offer more polished results. So what's the project? — children's story cassettes.

As a writer, I've been involved with a very broad cross section of publications, and written a great deal for the British arm of the Marvel comic company. I've noticed that a growing number of titles that I've written for have recently been appearing as cassette stories in bookshops, toy stores and even supermarkets as well. A friend of mine produced the written copy for one such release which has already sold over 15,000! I mention this to prove that, whilst on the face it, this idea may appear duff, it is in fact the most potentially lucrative one that I have presented so far, where sales and outlets are expanding at a furious pace. Couple this with the fact that you have probably got everything you need to make your own productions and you'll be cursing yourself for not thinking of the idea yourself.

The story
The first thing to do is come up with a good children's story. It should last for a maximum of 1000 words, all of which should be easy for children to understand. For instance, use things like 'he asked', as opposed to 'he enquired', and so on. The best age group to aim for is the under fives. For this group, the plot should be easy to follow — nothing complex or excessively verbose. It must have conflict, and above all, be fast moving, exciting and fun. You can portray fear or surprise by introducing stutters, like 'I-I c-can't s-see you!' he said. But remember, whatever you write, ensure that you bear the well known fiction writer's saying of 'cause and effect' in mind. Even young children have surprisingly logical minds, and if something happens in the story for no apparent reason, they *will* question it.

Cassette/books
The cassette/book concept is simple — a tape containing an exciting children's audio play, married up with a book of the script from which the play was produced. The idea is that the child listens to the tape whilst following the text in the accompanying book. Throughout the recording there are special tones recorded to indicate the turn of each page. These prompts make it very easy for a child to follow the action with both ears and eyes, making the package both entertaining and educational. The market for these products is growing steadily, with more and more companies jumping on the bandwagon. It's not just the independents either — large publishing groups are beginning to devote separate departments to cassette/books.

The actual writing of the stories for this market is easy, and the recordings can be great fun to do. The biggest fault lies in the fact that novices write their scripts as if they're only going to exist in book form.

You need to plan you story so that when it's acted out on tape, it sounds like a play. That means getting rid of all references to characters in the form of 'he said,' 'she said,' 'he replied hastily,' they shouted.' That's the most important point — if you've written the script properly then they're just not necessary. There are two ways to convey who is speaking and maintain clarity in dialogue. They are your golden rules:

1 Introduce your character prior to their speaking any dialogue, so that the listener knows who's speaking, e.g. Terry walked into the sitting room and sat down. 'What's for tea?'
2 At the end of a line of dialogue, tag on the person's name that it is directed at, e.g. Terry walked into the sitting room and sat down. 'What's for tea, Mum?'

You must avoid confusing the reader/listener — and most scripts of this nature are a compromise in some ways. Often the child will want to read the book without playing the cassette — and it must still make sense and employ correct English throughout. If you're still confused, buy a book on how to write plays. After all, this is a book about recording — not learning to write!

After you finish reading this section, try some cassette/book script alterations for yourself. Get any children's story book, and alter each story ready for cassette/book recording — it's best possible practice for you!

Children love effects. For instances; 'Kaboinnggg', 'Kaboinnggg', the floor bounced up and down like a trampoline! You should put as many of these in as possible. Finally, whatever you have happening throughout the story, make sure that the ending is a happy one.

The plot
I can visualise a lot of you sitting in your studios and staring at blank pieces of paper and scratching your head thinking 'it's all right for him'. So I thought that it would be a good idea to provide you with a sample plot that you can develop in whatever direction you like. It's hardly Enid Blyton standard, but it should give a start...

Paul lives in a big house with his sister Melisa, his Mum and Dad, and his teddy bear Neville. Paul's asleep in the bedroom, and is suddenly woken by Melisa who thinks she's heard burglars downstairs. They creep into the lounge to investigate and find their Mum's best silver candlestick has gone. Neville the bear comes alive and decides to secretly try to help. He sneaks out of the house in pursuit of the burglars, and has an exciting moonlight adventure which results in his getting the candlestick back. In the meantime Paul and Melisa have been trying to wake their parents. When they eventually come downstairs, the candlestick's back in its place, and Neville is laying in the armchair. Paul and Melisa think it must have all been a dream — but we know different!!

The recording
As I said earlier, all you need is a stereo recorder to simply put your story onto tape. However, if you have a four-track recorder, then this is the ideal opportunity to press it into service in a way that perhaps it hasn't been used in before. Let's look at the means of improving the story with your studio, one by one:

Atmosphere
After recording the narrative onto track 1, devote the second track to atmospheric effects. For instance, for the night-time adventure, you could add the hoot of an owl, the sound of the breeze rustling through the trees, and perhaps the chiming of a far off village clock. All these things, and hundreds more, are available on the excellent collection of BBC sound effects records. But it's often even more fun to make up your own 'on location'. You might even find that, at the right price, copies of your own recordings could be a saleable collection.

Improving the spoken effects in the narrative
Hopefully, you've put lots of 'boinnggs', 'kerbummps' and 'ka-blamms' into the narration of your story as I suggested earlier. Once the story is on tape, review each one and try to think of a sound to replace it, using whatever you have lying around. In one recent production, I persuaded the floor to bounce like a trampoline by using a DX synthesizer sound to replace the written 'boinnggs'. Chande-liers crashed to the ground by boosting the high EQ on the desk, and clattering a few music stands together, whilst simultaneously drop-ping a heavy book on the floor. The sound of someone putting their foot through a big bass drum was produced by ripping a piece of paper very close to a mic with a lot of bass EQ. And the sound of water dripping into a mysterious underground pool was created by record-ing a dripping tap in the kitchen, and then processing the result through a digital reverb.

I suggest that you arrange for all these effects to appear on track 3. On the final mix, all you will need to do is fade down the spoken 'kerflumps' etc. in the narration, and replace them with your effects, simply by sliding the fader up on track three. It is important that you record your effects to coincide exactly with those on the original narration. This is where a sampler can be extremely useful. Each effect can be recorded into the sampler first, and triggered from a keyboard at exactly the right moment. I use the Akai S612, but anything that allows a reasonable sampling time will do the job equally as well.

Theme music

A good little 'ditty' helps the action along. I use my Yamaha CX5 music computer for my compositions, which only need to last about 30 seconds or so, and can be stored on disk. Working in this way, I can change the instrument sounds and create lots of variations on the theme without undertaking further compositional work. This can then be transferred, at appropriate points, onto the fourth track of the story master.

If you don't have any computerised gear then you can make up some compositions using a separate master tape. Keep each instrument on a separate track. This can then be mixed in several different ways to produce a wide range of variations from the same recording. These mixes should be mastered onto a second machine and then dubbed back onto track 4 of the story master something like this:

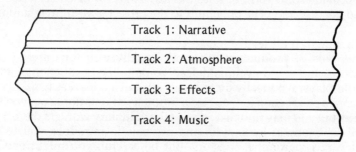

Figure 3.6 Four track format for cassette story project

The completed master can now be mixed and copied, as explained in Chapter 2.

Marketing and packaging

Your cassettes will realise the most sales if they're wrapped in a great-looking inlay card with the principal character from your story depicted on it. This is important! You really do need to make this look good if you want to have any chance of making volume sales. I think that it's a job well worth handing to a small art studio. Ideally, the finished printing should be in full colour, but if this turns out to be too costly then use a brightly coloured card, with a contrasting coloured ink. Children (and their parents) are much more likely to be attracted to the product if the inlay looks superb — well they can't see the sound can they? If you're feeling really ambitious then you could type up your story and produce it as a pamphlet to accompany the cassette. Most companies that do this put a bleep on the tape at the end of the page. This is so that the child can read along in the book, and know when to turn the page.

Contact all of the toy shops in your area and ask the manager to stock some of your tapes on a sale-or-return basis. Newsagents are another potential sales outlet, and there's bound to be at least one near you. Keep the purchase price modest so that you don't compete with professionals. I suggest that you sell for around £1.25. You will still make a good profit if you sell in volume, and use 'cut to length' cassettes bought from a bulk supplier.

Make sure that you include your address on the inlay card, and if you can afford it, set up a Freepost service (see the Post Office for details), so that existing customers can send for details of the rest of your titles without forking out any money. It's also a very good idea to provide some form of sales incentive like, for instance, 'buy four and get one free'. The only limit to the project is your imagination.

Where will it all lead?
This type of production can work equally well for different age groups, and could eventually lead you into the production of adult radio plays. An ideal way to break into such a market would be to record a production for your local hospital radio station. You won't be paid, but you may find that some of the voluntary workers there have full time jobs in local radio and are able to introduce you to the relevant programme directors. But be careful, you might end up producing 'The Archers!!'

From recording studio to dance studio

Dancing and music have always been linked, but have you ever thought of applying your production skills to make money from that fact? I have.

Not all dancing is simply mindless gyrations; there are in fact, still places where the whole process is carried out in a much more structured and orderly manner—dancing schools. For me they conjure up images of a cold hall where ageing spinsters try to regain there lost youth over a foxtrot or a waltz. But whilst establishments like this are doubtless still in existence somewhere, the majority of dancing schools nowadays have swung towards much more modern and exciting teaching programmes, aimed at encouraging the lucrative younger market.

Since the film 'Saturday Night Fever', dancing has been on a high, with people keen to learn how to 'strut their stuff' on the country's dancefloors in the most appealing way possible. Now dance schools use modern music! This is where you come in.

Contrary to what the Musician's Union think, discos are here to stay, and musicians, far from being put out of work because of their growth, can if they own some recording equipment, make more money than they were doing before. This section aims to provide realistic ways to achieve this.

I asked a dancing school in my hometown how they used modern music; 'We use it primarily for our disco dancing team', I was told. 'It's a bit awkward because we have to use sections of records, and attempt to segue from one to another. In competitions, we've often found that the deejay gets it wrong, and it wrecks the routine that we've spent months preparing.'

So that's problem number one. This could easily have been avoided if the school had its own specially recorded music. For one thing, the affair of linking records would be a thing of the past, and if original music was used then it could be provided on cassette without infringing the copyright laws that surround published music.

The first thing that you should do is look in your *Yellow Pages*, and contact all of the dancing schools near you to check whether they're experiencing similar problems. The chances are that, if they're involved in the modern competitive field, then they will be. Why not initially offer your services free, and produce a cassette for them that is precisely suited to their needs? If they like it then, as long as you set a realistic fee, they'll almost certainly use you further.

It's important that the music *is* suitable for them though, a cobweb covered reel laying in the dark vaults of your studio probably won't do. When I was asked to produce a routine recently, I actually visited the school and watched the dance team in action so that I could gauge the type of material required. If you've got a portable video then this is the ideal time to use it, as then you can sit at home in your studio and replay the movements when inspiration seems a world away.

It's also a good idea to ask what music the instructor is currently using, and use this as a basis for your own recordings (I don't mean copy). The length of the piece will be very important to the school because the team are given only a certain length of time on the floor. When I asked about his, another associated problem came to light. 'Using records, and linking them together, we are never able to get the 'big finish' to our routine that we'd like. The music simply fades out and we're left on the floor looking like lemons.'

With careful editing, you can time the piece to exactly what is required, and produce a big finish too. It seems that the only reason these dancing schools link records together is because they can't find one that has the necessary musical changes in the right place throughout it. Again, you can help.

But there are some gambles: ' Sometimes we travel to a competition only to find that another team is using the same piece of music as us, this creates even more competition, especially if the other team has come up with a slightly better routine. If we had our own music then this direct composition wouldn't occur. '

It really looks like there's a market out there ready to crack open doesn't it? It could also even offer you another chance to get your recordings onto discs too. Many competition halls don't have their own sound system and rely on an employed deejay. Think of the panic that would ensue if your team turn up with your recording on cassette, only to be told that there are no tape facilities available. Tell your prospective clients that you are able to supply the recordings on acetate discs to avoid such a disaster occurring, and make another reasonable profit.

It's not only in the finished competition that you can help, but during the long hard practice periods too. Dance instructors have to train their teams in each of the individual sections of the piece, and from what I've heard, they're fed up with trying to re-cue tapes or records throughout the sessions. It's tedious and time wasting they say. Using multitrack facilities you can produce your finished masters to exact specification, with a separate tape for each of the different sections of the dance. Each tape could feature the same section repeated over and over again so that it could be left running throughout the practice session unattended, leaving the teacher free to teach.

Obviously it's difficult to get complicated dance routines right first time at the correct speed, and so you could also provide slowed down versions of your recording, simply by tweaking the pitch control on your multitrack when you produce the master. But much better, if you've got access to it, is MIDI musical equipment. As mentioned earlier, I use a CX5 music computer and 'real-time' recording software. Working in this way, I can 'digitally record' the piece, and change both the instrumental sounds themselves, and the tempo of the piece without affecting the pitch in any way.

Submixes of the same piece of music are also very useful indeed. Certain members of the team are sometimes required to 'listen out' for specific sounds within the track. You can make this much easier for them if you provide mixes that accentuate their particular sounds in the mix. In addition, drum tracks on their own can also be of use in getting the team to move correctly to the beat without the distractions of the rest of the track.

All of these things are simple for owners of multitrack equipment, but seem totally amazing to people who know nothing about recording—i.e., dance teachers. Because of this, and because each school has a desire to win, you will, as long as your prices are realistic, be very much in demand. Remember, as soon as one competition finishes, work begins on the next one! You shouldn't find it too difficult to persuade the school to buy a stack of copies of your recording either. Each team member will then be able to practice at home, and consequently, practice sessions will prove much more fruitful. Don't forget to tell your prospective dancing school all this when you're touting for their business.

Even if you don't play an instrument yourself, there's bound to be a synthesizer player in the area with a drum machine who would jump at the chance of such exposure, even more so if he, or she, is paid a modest fee.

The music can be sold again and again. But I suggest that you give an undertaking to the dance school that you won't sell it again for a certain period of time though, to avoid the duplication of music in competition occurring too frequently. However, if it does, then it's not your fault that everyone thinks that your music is wonderful is it?

This type of service is straightforward to sell, because you're aiming at such a specialised target market. If the dancing schools near you are indifferent to your advances then you could try some specialist newspapers or magazines. But beware, a successful campaign in one of these could bring you in more work than you can readily handle. Here are a few markets that I've researched for you.

Dance and Dancers—established in 1950, this monthly features, amongst other things, reviews on modern dance. It could be the ideal place to book an advert. They can be contacted at 43b Gloucester Road, Croydon, CR0 2DH. The editor is John Percival, and the phone number is 01-689 3979.

Dancing Times—this monthly magazine deals with ballet and stage dancing as well, but it's worth getting hold of a copy and checking it out. They're based at Clerkenwell House, 45-47 Clerkenwell Green, London EC1R 0BE. The editor is Mary Clarke.

The IDTA (International Dance Teachers Association) could also be potentially lucrative. Members of this association have their own newspaper and this could form your number one choice.

So there we are, a big market definitely exists out there, and, as far as I know, it's virtually untapped. If you make the right approaches and ensure that your price is right, you could soon be helping a lot of people to 'get on down'.

Sell yourself—on cassette

Musicians reading this book will all want to be heard by a wider public and wish that their sounds were gracing the shelves of their local audio store. Impossible? No! There is a way to achieve this—and make a profit too—produce a cassette.

It's easy to make music available in this way, and it has considerable advantages over the more costly procedure of cutting a disc. Any cassettes that don't sell aren't wasted—they can be re-used—unlike records which, when the sales dry up, become nothing more than vinyl mountains in group member's attics.

With a cassette-based product, especially if you produce it yourself, you are in a position to quickly manufacture exactly the right amount to feed your market. Also, the programme material can be updated at any time to reflect changes in a current line-up or set. In contrast, expensive batches of vinyl pressings start at 250 and are 'unalterable'.

Cassettes are ultimately the most flexible and cheapest way to proceed as a first foray into music production. They may not be as ego-boosting as seeing your name on your own record, but they will enable you to make a profit—a feat almost impossible with a small batch of discs.

The first consideration is, of course, the recording of a suitable master tape. This can either be entrusted to a reputable recording studio, or be handled yourself. The latter option is, in my view, the most satisfying and certainly much more fun. It's been made possible by the recent rapid advances in home recording technology. These days, four channel cassette based machines, such as the excellent Fostex X15, can be bought for around £250, or hired from music shops for as little as £10 per day. Working with such equipment, you are freed from the creatively-stifling, clock watching syndrome associated with 'pay by the hour' recording studios—after all, you must have recording equipment, or you wouldn't have bought this book, would you?

Whichever you choose, it's important to end up with a good quality master recording produced on the correct format for copying. If you're careful then, should your cassette release be the success that you hope for, the same master could be used as a basis for subsequent disc pressings.

If you're using a cassette-based machine at home, then the easiest method is to mixdown onto a second standard hi-fi machine, loaded with a quality tape such as TDK's SAX. With studio recordings, it's well worth arranging for the production of an industry standard 15 i.p.s half-track reel-to-reel master in addition to a cassette based one.

Duplication

If you don't want to do the copies yourself, use a specialist cassette duplication company. They are extremely useful when large quantities are required quickly, and are also an excellent source of supply for blank 'cut to length' cassettes. As a rough guide, a C40 would cost an average of 40p from such a supplier—much cheaper than buying from the shops. Most such companies will also offer you a real time copying option at a slightly higher price. The theory is that, as each cassette is duplicated at normal speed, the quality will be better—but this depends on other factors, such as type of machines used too. The cost will be inflated, because the operation takes more time per unit than high speed. If your project requires only a limited number of cassettes, then you could copy your own using conventional hi-fi decks (as we've seen).

Your music cassette won't sell easily without an attractive inlay card, so you need to turn your attention to designing suitable artwork. A short run of less than 100 won't warrant the expense of the services of a printer. It's much more cost effective to go it alone. One of the easiest methods is to use a black and white photograph of the band in conjunction with some suitable dry transfer lettering.

For this particular project, it's best to avoid side labels—they will prevent professional looking re-use of the cassettes in the event of them not selling. However, a sticker informing the purchaser of the *a* and *b* sides is, of course, a must.

Selling your cassettes

Once again, local music shops make good sales outlets. Most musicians have a favourite shop that they've spent considerable sums of money in over the last few years. Such shops will find it difficult to refuse a request from a valued customer to stock a few cassettes on a sale or return basis. (Sale or return means that you hand a batch of cassettes to the shop, but they don't pay you anything until they've sold them—they return any that they can't sell.)

Record shops are another worthwhile outlet, although most will require a hefty percentage for any sales that they may make. Major national chains often have a central buying office in London, or will at least have to okay such ventures with head offices etc. To avoid this 'red tape', and to get face-face with the decision maker, try local independent dealers first.

If you're a musician in a band you have a captive audience (almost!) at your own gigs. Why not build the cassette into your inter-song patter? 'this next number's from our new cassette, available at the door!'

A good many small radio stations welcome 'local news' stories. Send a letter to every station in your vicinity explaining how you have produced your own release. Give it a good angle—'no one had faith in our music so we put our money where our mouth was and it's paid off,' or 'we were all unemployed but wanted to make an effort to earn some money in the only way we knew how,' etc. Ensure that you intimate that the product is selling in vast quantities—more than your wildest dreams. Tell them that you are surprised at how much media interest it has created (even if it hasn't). But take special care not to sound big headed—close with a line such as 'We think our relations must be buying them all up!'

An angle is the most important key to your product's success and can't be overstressed. Why not offer to give a percentage of the profits from every tape sale to a charity that's currently in the news? It will probably guarantee you exposure in the local media and give the band a good image too.

Most areas have several local newspapers. These must be contacted and offered a story. Adverts to support any editorial that you manage to obtain can work well. If possible, such adverts should be on the same page as your editorial. These can either be in form of 'available from' or the 'buy off the page', mail order type, (you'll need to sign a special blue PPA form for these—the newspaper will provide it).

Incentives are very often effective in promoting sales. However, you need to think of ones that are valuable to the public, but don't directly cost you any money. One such idea is to slip a voucher in with each cassette, offering a discount from the entry free of one of your forthcoming gigs. It may swell the crowd at your next gig, and sell more tapes too—it works both ways!

You could also get any fans of the band to act as salesmen for you. They will want to see you do well and will probably be only too pleased to help. Give them the added incentive of free admission to your next gig if they achieve a certain target, or even put them on a commission, and you will have harnessed a very successful sales force indeed.

Every advertising poster that you produce to publicize forthcoming gigs should mention the tape. A copy should also be distributed free to all mobile discos—they often have a cassette deck within their console.

Hit the charts

Often there's a shop in the city that provides the figures for a local paper's music chart. If you can find out which one this is, ensure that they have a good supply of tapes, and make everyone go to that shop to buy their copies within a certain week (an incentive here will help). If all your sales are channelled through this one outlet for a while, then there's a good chance of the tape making a brief showing on the local chart. This in itself will create publicity and provide another angle for a local press story 'Independently produced cassette from local band makes the Bodlhampton charts!'

Paperwork is something that most people find boring, but it is an essential part of the sales effort. You need to know precisely how many units each of your sales outlets has, when they were supplied, and how they are selling.

Make a separate sheet for each outlet. This should be headed with a name, address, phone number and a personal contact name. Under this, write the date and number of units supplied. Make two copies and ensure that both parties sign the document. Hand the original over to the shop and retain a copy for your files. Act in a businesslike way, and explain that you will return in a month to check on sales and collect any money due. On this return call, ensure that you have adequate small change with you to ensure a professional 'to the penny' collection of your profits. Also, bring a fresh stock of cassettes with you—if your product has sold well then the shop will be keen to re-stock.

In contrast, be prepared also to remove stock from shops if necessary. If one particular outlet is repeatedly selling out of tapes, and another has only sold one or two, it may be necessary to move the slow moving stock into the fast moving outlet. Otherwise, you may find that to keep the good outlet going you have to produce another run of cassettes. This is not the best economic policy when there's an unsold pile in another outlet. If your paperwork is kept up to date then situations like this will be easy to spot.

Going on the record

Many of the points mentioned in the previous section—Sell yourself—on cassette, also apply to putting your work, or your client's work, onto disc. There are plenty of custom record pressing plants that specialize in turning tapes into records for anyone who has the necessary capital available.

What do you need?
Most pressing plants prefer to work from reel to reel tapes, recorded at a speed of ether 7½, or 15 inches per second. This form of master affords much better quality than the humble cassette. If you are embarking on a single release, then it's well worth mixing your multitrack master down onto this format (although some plants will grudgingly accept cassettes), even if you have to hire a suitable machine to do so. Ask for a stereo half track tape deck at your friendly (?) local music shop.

Where do you find the people to do the job?
All of the major national music weeklies have an advertisement section near the back of their publications. Most of the principal pressing plants advertise here, and will be happy to provide you with rates on request.

How much will it cost?
This depends largely on quantity—the more that you order, the cheaper it becomes. Pressings of 10,000 often have a unit price of just 16p or so, whereas shorter runs could mean an outlay of £1 or more per disc. The shortest run that I've ever managed to persuade a pressing plant to agree to is 250, and so you should plan your release as an ongoing promotion, as opposed to a quick profit plan. If you or your client is gigging regularly, then a period of about three months should be enough for you to sell this amount at a small profit—less than cassettes, but with much more prestige that could ultimately improve your image, and allow you to increase your rates accordingly—and that's the bottom line!

The options
For the ambitious, then there's the 12 inch single in a picture sleeve, or, for the more prolific, the full length album. However, if you do decide on more than one song per side of your record, then you must ensure that your master tape has a portion of coloured leader tape spliced between each track. This will enable the pressing plant to provide you with the familiar banding on the finished disc that is so essential to accurate cueing.

As far as printing is concerned, I would recommend that you do without a logo on the centre label (thus avoiding printing plate costs), and, in the case of 7 inch singles, simply arrange for the disc to be supplied in conventional paper sleeves—those with the hole in the middle that the label peeps through—remember? This will further reduce unnecessary printing costs, which have a nasty habit of running into hundreds of pounds if you let them.

Acetates
If you only want a few discs, perhaps to use as initial demos for one purpose or another, then you could resort to direct cut acetates. These are made without recourse to many of the complicated pressing processes that surround conventional discs, and can therefore be supplied in very small quantities (less than 10!). The drawbacks are that these discs are fragile, and only have a limited playing life before the crackles become louder than the music. As well as this, they're very brittle, rather like the old 78s. They're also very expensive for what they are—to make it worth its while, the pressing plant will normally charge around £10 per copy!

Marketing
If your client feels unable to shift a batch of records at his gigs alone, then before he commits himself to a disc pressing, go along with him to several local record shops and enquire whether they will be willing to sell your discs. Most will be sympathetic to the cause, but will nevertheless require a commission on sales. Your client must ensure that he still realises a profit after this figure has been deducted. With short runs of 250 or so, the margin may not make it viable. Perhaps it would be better to go for 500? Work out a break even point, assess the market, then decide. Working with your clients in this way, they will learn to trust you, and won't feel that they're being 'ripped off' in the unhappy event of sales not reaching the expected level.

What can go wrong?
I can only talk from personal experience, but on my first single, I got the batch back, only to find that the holes were slightly off-centre and the disc exhibited the sounds of a drunken reveller at an all-night disco This was a clear-cut case of the faulty manufacture, but the pressing plant like to blame the cutting suite, and so it goes on. However, we were eventually supplied with a new batch.

The only other problem I've encountered was on a single that arrived with the labels stuck on the wrong sides. The pressing plant maintained that it was my fault, as, although the tape was clearly labelled, I had put the B side first on the master, which confused everybody. Bear that one in mind!

If you release a record and it's successful in your area, both you, as the producer, and the artist, will be remembered for a long time, and get a lot of free publicity. Be prepared to do no more than break even, and you will have great fun. Try to be rich and you'll have a nightmare! On a national level? Well that's a different matter entirely!

Picture music

Every visual image that we see, with just a few exceptions, includes a musical backdrop—video, slides, film and television. They all rely on music to augment the images presented. One of the easiest markets to break into in this field is the tape/slide presentation. This is where information on an audio tape is used to control several slide projectors. Most producers of these programmes accept that the music is just as important as the slides, and are always on the look out for something different. The people who produce these epics aren't unapproachable either. Your Yellow Pages will probably provide you with the phone numbers of several that are in your immediate area, handling productions for local businesses, etc. If you can get in with them, then it's quite likely that they'll begin to use you for other projects too. Most of these small producers can't exist on slide/tape productions alone, and so they produce videos as well—they use music too!

For a slide/tape presentation, the producer first has to define his objectives and decide what impression he wants to create with the audience. He usually ends up with a treatment that includes both the slides and the music. For big productions, the budget can extend to the writing of original songs. This where you can come in, especially if you're a multi-instrumentalist. What you should do is send a demo tape of some of your original music to all of the local producers of video and slide/tape programmes, bearing in mind that material for such productions should play a supporting role, and not overshadow the visuals.

Producers can use music from the commercial charts, or from specialist music libraries, but the fees involved in clearing these for public performance can be very restrictive. You should offer your services on a 'buy out' basis. You work closely with the producer, then go away and compose, produce and record the music. When it's finished, it's sold to the producer for a once-only fee that you both agree to. You relinquish all copyright in the piece, and give the producer the right to use it on as many productions as he likes without paying you more money. Seems unfair on you? Well, to an extent, it is, but you are competing with professional music libraries and chart hits! It's unlikely that you can win on musical terms, so you've got to win on financial ones instead. They're the ones that most producers are most interested in anyway.

There's not much else to say, simply try it and hope for the best. I did exactly that, and found myself composing music for TVS commercials. Some pieces were produced way back in 1983, and are still on TV some five years later. That producer certainly got his money's worth out of me!

Deejay jingles

We're into the age of the hi-tech deejay. Today's record-spinners want to stand out from their contemporaries. One way in which they can do this cost-effectively is to use customized jingles. You could easily produce these for them!

To begin with, all you need is a mic, a voice and a tape recorder. It's a simple matter of hollering enthusiastic comments into the microphone that can be used at appropriate moments during gigs. Whilst this is initially good fun, and using them gives the bored deejay with a crowd of wallflowers something to do, it soon becomes obvious that more elaborate productions would be better.

Add effects
Re-read Chapter 2, and try out some of the effects mentioned. Using the sound on sound recording method to produce multi-layered jingles. You may find it worth using a reverb unit and a digital delay to add that professional sheen to any vocals. Countless creative possibilities are then on offer. How about using the delay to create a 'Fred's Roadshow-show-show' jingle? The repeat echo will gradually fade to nothing through the opening bars of the deejay's next record.

Add a musical instrument
All you need is a simple keyboard. You select a modern hi-tech sound to use as a background wash for the jingle, and then add an effects-laden vocal track. You will find that a more or less continuous mid-range synthesizer backing sound patch will mask much of the inevitable hiss build up, and perhaps allow you to squeeze an extra overdub.

If a sequencer and drum machine are on hand then you will be in the enviable position of being able to digitally compose and pre-record your musical 'bed'—most modern equipment has a special interface called MIDI (I mentioned it earlier). It facilitates synchronized link-ups with keyboards, sequencers and drum machines. Working with such equipment, you can often do the whole jingle in one take. After programming the sequencer, you can enter a pattern into the drum machine. This done, simply set your first tape machine running in the record mode, and hit the start button on the sequencer. Whilst the pattern is running add your vocal part. It's all done in one go. No fuss, no bother—and no loss of quality either. But do ensure that you have mixed the music bed down low enough to allow the vocal to be heard.

Cueing
I find that it's useful to record a bleep about two seconds before the jingle begins. This will aid the deejay's cueing when on gigs. He simply listens for the bleep, then holds the cassette deck on pause until the jingle is required. Make sure that there's an adequate gap between the jingles on the tape to make this easy for the deejay.

A four track jingle plan

Whilst all home recordists will have their own favourite way of planning tracks, the following will serve as a basic course of action for producing a saleable jingle using multitrack.

Tracks 1 and 2
Earlier on, I discussed the use of a MIDI linked sequencer and drum machine. The same approach could be used with multitrack. This time, however, the outputs from each machine are sent to separate tracks of the recorder.

Connect the sequencer (or keyboard) output to track 1 input. Run the pattern and adjust the input volume for track 1 accordingly. Achieve the highest possible level to mask hiss. Most multitracks have bass and treble controls on each of their inputs. These should be adjusted to your liking. They will affect the actual recording going onto tape. This time you don't have to allow for degradation in tonal quality as you proceed—there won't be any.

The drum machine, which if linked via MIDI will trigger when the sequencer is started, should be connected to track 2. Once the independent levels and tonal characteristics are set up to your liking, set the multitrack to record. You can monitor the recording through headphones connected direct to the machine, or by plugging its line output into a conventional hi-fi amplifier.

Track 3
Rewind the tape to where you started, and put tracks 1 and 2 into the playback mode.

In this example, we will record a vocal onto track 3. Set up a microphone, and connect it to the machine's track 3 input. Once again, you will be able to adjust the tone to your liking. For this operation it's best to monitor through headphones. If you are using speakers, then feedback may occur. Also, with speakers, it's likely that some of the other tracks being monitored will spill onto this third one, getting picked up unwanted via the microphone—remember leakage?

Put track 3 into the record mode, and leave tracks 1 and 2 in playback. Through the headphones you'll hear the sequencer and drum machine, and you'll be able to deliver your vocal at the correct point in your production.

Once track 3 is recorded, rewind the tape and put this into the playback mode too. Now listen to your efforts. If you feel you could have made a better job of your vocal, it's a simple matter of re-recording the third track. The sequencer and drum machine on tracks 1 and 2 will be unaffected.

Track 4
How about using this as a sound effects track? You could feed an output from one of your record decks into this track's input. BBC sound effects records are great fun to use, and whilst monitoring the other three tracks in the way described, you could add explosions, thunder or 101 other effects on cue, simple by spinning the record in at the required point. The advantage is, if you go wrong, you can do it again without damaging the other three tracks. Now take a look at the section on Mixdown in Chapter 2 for guidance on how to create your saleable finished product.

Using a multitrack, you can produce a handful of different jingles from the same recording, simply by varying the mix—using different effects, fading certain tracks in and etc. In fact, you are working in a similar way to the producers who construct 12 inch mixes of hit records.

There are many useful contacts in the disco world to be found in a monthly magazine, called 'JOCKS'.

4 How to sell your services

Okay, now you've got the ideas. But that's not enough. To make money, you've got to know how to sell those recording services to the public—cheaply and efficiently to maximize your profits. In Chapter 3 we looked at some brief marketing start points. Now we'll get down to the nitty-gritty.

USP

This stands for unique selling point. Your USP is the difference, or the edge that you've got over your competitors. It's important to define your USP, otherwise you'll find it difficult to sell effectively against any competition that might rear its head in your area. To find out what your USP is, you've got to ask yourself the question—Why do people buy from me?

It's a good idea to spend some time sitting and thinking, writing down every answer to the question that you can think of. First of all, typical old answers will flow—I'm the best, I'm the cheapest, and so on. But gradually, these superficial answers will gain more body and depth— keep thinking and writing. Soon you'll begin to develop a picture of why you think you're the best, why you're making your services cheaper, etc.

When you've gone as far as you can possibly go towards answering the question, and your piece of paper is crammed full, fetch a new piece, and head it Why do people buy from my competitors? and start all over again. Again, the common answers will surface in your mind first—price, their advertising is more effective, and so on. Then you start digging deeper: Which of my competitors beats me on advertising, and why? Which competitors do I beat, and why? Using this form of creative thinking, both of your lists will grow and grow. As they do, it will become clear that you have some advantages over your competitors. Those advantages are what you need to capitalize on, they are your USP's. Unfortunately, you'll also find that you've uncovered some weaknesses in your services. But now that these are clearly defined, they can be dealt with swiftly.

Beating your competitors

There are many people in your area who want your services. Your job, if you want to make money from home recording, is to find them, and do so before your competitors do! The first thing to get right is your approach — be positive. So what if you've only got a four track, and your competitor's got a fully equipped mobile eight track studio in a new van? There are lots of advantages in your service. You should already know them if you've explored your USP carefully. You've got to become Sherlock Holmes of your town—detecting business.

Good detectives are inquisitive. You need to build up a file of information on the people that you're aiming at and search them out, ask them questions, get them to lead you on to further potential customers (I'll call them prospects from now on, because that's what they are — prospective customers). You also need to have a carrot to dangle in front of your prospect when you've found him. Something that will be of use to him, something that will encourage him to use your service above all others — your USP.

Handling complaints

Complaints, whilst not something that you want very often, can actually help you. If dealt with promptly and efficiently, the customer is impressed, and mentions how good you are at dealing with problems to friends. If you haven't got a complaints procedure, then the customer is likely to get irate and, even when eventually satisfied, rant and rave to friends about how bad you are.

When you get a complaint, do the following: thank the customer for bringing the problem to your notice, and for giving you the opportunity to put things right. Say that you're sorry he or she's been upset—but don't apologise, you don't know whose fault it is yet. Now get the full story down on paper without interrupting, arguing or justifying. Finally, tell the customer what action you're going to take, form an agreement, and do it, quickly.

Tiny complaints will grow into bigger ones if you try to ignore them—they won't go away. You need to deal with them straightaway with a smile.

Dealing with rumour spreading

Unprofessional competitors will sometimes spread rumours about your services in a bid to divert business away from you, and into their hands. You need a plan to deal with this before it gets out of hand. Find out what the rumours are, then bring them right out into the open, tell your customers about them, and prove that they're untrue. Make a point of mentioning rumours to prospects. For example, if a rumour is going around that your recordings are of inferior quality and swamped with background noise, offer to play some of your tapes and prove the competitors wrong. Once proved wrong, the rumour can be turned around and will work to your advantage. Laugh about it and say to your prospect 'You see, such-and-such has to resort to underhanded tactics to gain business. It's pathetic isn't it. We'd never stoop so low!' The prospect will agree with you, and the other business will be in his black books for evermore as being a shady distrustful outfit. Simple, isn't it?

Incoming phone calls

Most of your business will be generated in this way. This is the point at which your prospects will first encounter you and form an instant opinion. It's absolutely vital to make that first impression a good one. So many businesses are hopeless on the phone, and employ secretaries that, because they're ill-informed about the company, don't know, and don't care about the customer.

The prospect's requirements must be properly listened to and complied with where possible. The voice that the caller hears mustn't be irritating or depressing. So, whenever the telephone rings, whatever mood you're in, SMILE before you pick up the receiver. Have a pad of paper and a pen next to the phone, and take full details of the call, then file it. When you pick up the phone, sing out your name - 'Hello, this is Clive Brooks. How can I help?' So many small business just pick up the phone and mumble 'hello'. That's no good at all!!

It's also important to make sure that any other members of your household know the phone drill. It sounds totally unprofessional if your mum/dad/wife/girlfriend answers and says 'yeah, whadd'ya want.'

How much?

You've told your prospect all your services, he thinks that they're, great, then you tell him the price!... How much? All your selling effort ruined in two words. You've got to remain positive, and be *proud* of your prices, because you know in detail how and why they're justified. Your customer wouldn't have griped at the price at all if you'd put over all the benefits and justification for using you properly in the first place.

But in this day and age, customers like to test their suppliers, to see if they are negotiable on price. It's all a game really, but it's one that you *must* win! Ask with sincerity; 'Don't you think that quality is worth that much?' If your prospect laughs and says something like 'That's not the point,' then retort with 'Just like any business that puts quality first, we have to protect our margins. Otherwise it wouldn't be long before the quality of our service began to suffer, would it?'

If he comes back with, 'Yes but it's too expensive,' then ask 'How much too expensive?' Once you know this, you can tailor your service to his requirements, without resorting to discounts (they should be avoided where possible). For example, if it's a tape copying service, offer the product on cheaper tapes, or if it's a wedding recording, offer the edited highlights on a 7 inch disc instead of the 12 inch LP — or if that's still too dear, then offer to supply on cassette for a reduced price. Whatever happens, you must get your prospect to define the difference between the price you're asking, and the price he can afford/is willing to pay. Without this figure, negotiations are impossible. If he's genuine, and does want to use your services, then getting your figure out of him should be easy—after all, you're offering to help—you're on his side. If he's reluctant to give a figure, then he's probably just trying to get out of using you anyway. Let him go, there are plenty more prospects where he came from—if you're a good detective!

Finally, if your prospect has four or five quotations in front of him, one of which is yours, and looks up and says 'You are the most expensive!' simply say 'Yes, we are' then keep quiet. After a few seconds your prospect will probably say 'I suppose that's because you're the best!' to which you reply: 'Yes— absolutely right!' Then go on to justify why, without resorting to slagging off the competition.

Remember: *You're not selling prices, you're selling your services: quality, value, satisfaction and many other things that make it worth paying a higher price for.*

Demonstrations

With recording, most of the time you'll be selling sound. That's a difficult commodity for anyone to judge without a demonstration. So, where possible, you need to set these up, either at your home studio, or, if necessary, at the prospect's home. The secret of success in demonstrations is to follow the format 'tell - show - tell'.

You should break your demonstration into pieces. Tell them about the service that they're interested in, show them your product, by playing a tape, and then tell them the next bit. At the start, tell the prospect all the things that you propose to show him, play the tape, then explain each of the things that you promised. Recap on everything the prospect has seen and heard, then ask whether he'd like you go through anything again, or even the whole demonstration. Finally, see if there are any questions that need answering. Oh, and don't forget to push your USP's!

When you're going through your demonstration, try to use FAB—Feature, Advantage, Benefit. It should dovetail into your USP's. It's all too easy to go through a demonstration explaining all the features of your service, but forgetting to explain the advantages and benefits that the prospect can derive from these features.

'I'd like to think about it'

Most people worry about making decisions. If your prospect says 'I'd like to think about it,' then try the following. 'Okay, I know you won't be wasting your time giving this a lot of thought. But just in case I've missed something out, precisely what aspects of the service do you want to think over? - Is it the recording quality?'

You've got to get that last question in without a pause before your prospect says, 'The whole thing!' The idea is to get him to say 'no' to a whole list of things, like Is it the number of tracks? Is it the availability of digital reverb? Is it the delivery time?

You'll probably get a couple of yes's. Deal with them to the prospect's satisfaction, then ask 'Are these the only things that are worrying you?' If he says 'No' then deal with any other points to his satisfaction, then say 'Well, if there's nothing that I've missed, can we call it a deal then?'

Don't become a high-pressure salesman, that's not the idea at all, no one likes those. But *Do* use the special techniques presented in this chapter to help you. They're very powerful, and they *do* work!

5 A guide to good publicity

Advertising is expensive, and sometimes it's difficult to justify, especially when you see all your profits disappearing into a few printed lines, and the telephone never rings. However, there is a way around this uninviting state of affairs, and it's free publicity, or, to give it its correct title—public relations.

Basically, PR is your total publicity package into which all the other components, such as advertising, sales promotion and image, fit logically. Good publicity is good PR, and good PR is good publicity! It's a means of communicating with the people who need to know about and understand your services, to enable you to succeed. If you can win their goodwill, you'll establish a well-known image and soon have a good reputation. A good piece of editorial in a local newspaper or on radio can stimulate enquiries for you to follow up, and it need not cost you a penny!

It's important to build a good reputation for yourself fast. People's trust and confidence must be obtained and maintained. You don't want to appear to your potential clients as a crafty fly-by-night organization just out for a quick buck. The art of PR is to make people aware of the special qualities, interest and scope of your services, so that they come to know you better, and appreciate you more than your competitors.

Image

Image is the impression which others have of you, according to what they've experienced, or what they've heard. It's often confused with identity, which is your uniqueness, range of services and the way you actually go about things. Both Image and Identity are very important, and the sooner you establish good ones, the better. Are you misunderstood? Do potential customers understand what you're trying to sell them? Do you deserve wider recognition for any of your achievements? Doing something positive about questions like these is 'image building'.

You need to work out some key features—ones that you want to put across to the outside world. Pick the simplest, strongest features of your recording services and write a short profile about your venture in about 50 words. Frankly, if you can't describe your recording services to the outside world yourself, then nobody else will be able to either! Be honest, don't write down any lies, and don't try to pretend that you're something that you're not. What you come up with will be the nucleus of what you must aim to put in people's minds—your image.

Your PR effort should extend to your suppliers too. The company that supplies you with tape and cassettes will want to feel that you're a reputable individual, both credible and creditworthy. It's up to you to develop that image—no one else will do it for you. Make every effort to involve them in any publicity that comes your way and perhaps they'll do the same for you someday. Goodwill with everyone is really important if you want to build a successful recording business quickly.

Getting your message heard

You need to find out where your target audience gets its information from. Where would you look if you wanted to find out about recording services? Do you depend on the local paper? Yellow pages? Radio adverts? or whatever. Ask yourself, and also ask your existing customers, perhaps in the form of a questionnaire.

Personally, I've always advertised in local papers. They exercise a strong community influence, and fulfil the role of the local gossip circle. The information in there is relied on by the majority of people in your area, whatever their interests. Advertising here is cheaper than the dailies, and the circulation is more targeted to your requirements—and what's more, there's a chance of editorial coverage too.

When booking advertising, ask for discounts and you'll usually get them, especially if you are booking space on a regular basis. Also, find out exactly where the circulation of the paper is biggest, and ask for a readership survey sheet. This will give you valuable information on whether this particular publication is reaching the age group/type of person that you require, etc.

The advertising 'copy' itself (the words you use in the ad) is very important, especially if you're relying on classifieds to get your message across. There are very few words at your disposal, so each one must count. I've found that it's best to avoid putting an address, for security reasons, to save space, and also to control replies. If there's only a phone number, then all of your potential business will flow through this channel, and you can be prepared for it and plan precisely what to say to prospective clients.

News

To get that editorial coverage, you'll have to do something newsworthy. But can you recognise what makes a good news story, in the way that a newspaper editor can? In a nutshell, news is what the casual browsing reader, who doesn't much care about anything in particular, will take the trouble to read. Basically news falls into two categories, good news and bad news—that's all journalists are interested in. They like exclusive stories to try to keep ahead of their rivals. However, before you offer a specific publication your story, ask yourself whether an exclusive in one paper would really be better for your business than several smaller pieces in smaller circulation local papers.

To help you get started on the road to making news, and hence free advertising, here are a few ideas.

1 Launching of a unique new recording service.
2 Examples of how you've helped a customer by using your skills.
3 How you've done something for a famous local character or special customer.
4 An interesting end-use for one of your recordings.
5 Help given by you in an emergency.
6 Participation in a forthcoming exhibition.
7 What an interesting or unusual visitor has to say about your recording services—a good quote!
8 A link forged between your business and another local one.
9 A stunt arranged by yourself to attract local TV, press and radio.
10 The numbers game, when the umpteenth recording is completed, person helped, etc.
11 Review of a year's activities.
12 An announcement of unique future plans.
13 Sponsoring of a project, particularly if it's unusual or the first of its kind.

People

No news is news without people. Readers much prefer stories with some kind of human element attached to them. Even earthquakes don't make good news unless there are people involved—just watch the TV news tonight if you don't believe me! For this reason, ensure that any news stories that you concoct have this essential element connected with them—it works!

Press releases

Writing background briefing notes for the media is just common sense. You've got to put down on paper all you want to say, clearly and concisely, without missing out anything important. Steer clear of jargon and cliches. The first sentence is the most important one, as it must summarise exactly what your services are all about, and encapsulate the whole story in a short punchy way. To help you, look at any newspaper story. They all use this technique, beginning with factual summaries that encourage you to read on. As a guide, your press release should be based on the following:

What has happened or is about to happen.
Who was involved or is about to be involved.
Where?
When?
How?
Why?—anything that gives extra credibility to the story.

When you're writing a press release, use short sentences and simple words, avoiding long paragraphs. Type it up on A4 paper, double-spaced with wide margins each side. This gives the editors plenty of room to make any changes that they see fit. The finished piece should be no longer than two pages, and should include the date.
Here's a useful checklist:

Is there a topical news story to tell?
If others are involved, have they given their permission to be included in the story?
What has, or is about, happen?
Who was involved and why?
Where did, or where will it happen?

Is a press release really necessary—or would a phone call to a local paper be enough?
Would an accompanying photo help the story—is the event visual?

Bad news

Occasionally, you may find yourself appearing in a paper because you've made a mistake, failure or had some kind of accident or misunderstanding with someone. If this happens, don't shy away from it—meet any reporters that come your way, and give them the full story from your side. That way, gossip and rumours can easily be nipped in the bud. It's very rarely good policy to hide from the press. Simply exercise all the tact and discretion you can. Refusing to comment may lead journalists to come to their own conclusions, often with disastrous consequences.

Exhibitions

Occasionally, an exhibition will be staged locally that is worth taking part in—perhaps a communications display in which you could show your answerphone message recording service, or a wedding show, at which you could display your wedding LP service, and so on. However, taking part can be a hard and expensive slog with no guaranteed rewards. The questions to answer before you take the plunge are:

1 Are potential customers likely to attend the exhibition on a reasonable scale?
2 On what scale is it necessary for you to take part. How large a stand will you have to occupy, and what will it cost?
3 Can you afford it? And even if you can, would the money be better spent in alternative advertising?
4 Can you man the stand throughout the exhibition without losing/missing other commitments?

Good public relations is largely a matter of common sense. It's down to earth and practical really. The wish to look vaguely like a good neighbour is not enough. That wish has to be transferred into specific initiatives, establishing direct lines of contact with local decision formers—the secret is know and be known!
It all comes down to the following:

What are we trying to achieve?
Who are we aiming at?
What do we want to say?
How do we get it across?
Did it work?

Finally, here's a checklist to help with generating publicity. Use it!

What makes your recording services different?
Have you got a clear plan of action and objectives?
Do you know what image you are striving to put over to others?
Does your chosen image relate to your real image?
Is your base easy to find?
Is everyone who answers the phone well-briefed and efficient?
Do you know what media are important to you?
Do you have good up-to-date photos to support any possible editorial?
Do you know, by name, the people in the media who would talk about or write about your recording services?
Can you handle interviews with confidence?

6 Hiring out your studio

Sound recording is the cheapest that it has ever been, and you're getting more for your money in terms of sophistication and quality than ever before. This is one of the reasons that home studio recordists are setting up their own commercial studios—from back bedrooms to back gardens, rooms across the country are being transformed into electronic jungles—jungles into which the home recordist, after reading this far in the book, should easily be able to attract paying customers.

But before you put the book down and rush off, *wait*! On a gloomier note, it has to be said that most projects of this nature are doomed to failure at the point in which they begin to succeed—the money starts coming in, and suddenly *bang*! There are tax forms to fill in, public liability insurance to worry about, advertising to budget for, and so on. If you go into recording full time, than you'll have plenty of hassles that are absent in a day job. But you can do anything you want as long as you put your mind to it—it's just that sometimes you need a little extra guidance, that's all. That's what this chapter is all about— a sort of 'Ask Clive' advice column!

The recording venue

Can you run a studio from home? That's the first question to answer. No-one is going to stop you and a few friends using the recording equipment that you've bought. It's when your friends start to become your clients that problems can begin to occur. The first thing to do is consult the deeds of your house. Sometimes there is a clause that forbids business use of the premises. But that's usually placed there to stop mechanics from starting up car repair workshops next door, or obnoxious industrial plants that will generally ruin the area, etc. On some deeds, there is a sub-clause that permits 'learned or artistic activities'—this could give you the opportunity that you need.

Basically, you must prove to your local planning office that your proposed studio will not create nuisance problems. The two main concerns are usually those of noise, and parking. If these requirements can be met, then you'll often get the go ahead for a trial period—but check first, not only with the authorities, but with your family as well! It should also be pointed out that the home must remain a dwelling house, and not be given over exclusively to business use . Your local authorities will tell you what the balance between business and dwelling is. I strongly suggest that you contact them. They're usually quite willing to advise, and the government is keen to help the small business—to an extent.

Enterprise allowance

It's quite possible that you could be eligible for a £40 per week grant to help get you started in business. There's a scheme available, run by the Manpower Services Commission. You can find out more about it by contacting your local jobcentre, or by dialling 100, speaking to the operator and asking for Freephone Enterprise. So what's the catch? Well, you need to have been unemployed for eight weeks or more, and must be in receipt of unemployment and/or supplementary benefit. You also need to be able to raise £1000 yourself, be between 18 and 65 years of age, and be willing to work a minimum of 37 hours per week. If you're keen to take the plunge into recording in a serious way, then it's easy to make yourself eligible, and you'll be mad not to take advantage of such a valuable offer—I wish the Enterprise Allowance Scheme had been available when I started. I used to go weeks without a client, and struggle to afford advertising in my local paper.

Business premises

If it turns out that, after contacting your local planning people, you are refused permission to operate at your home, then all is not lost. Throughout the country, many private enterprise schemes are cropping up. These are run by commercial developers, keen to make money, but also keen to assist small businesses. Most of these are housed in small development parks—one near me is in a converted seed mill. The buildings are split into many small room-sized units, which are rented out to small businesses.

Renting a unit is much easier than trying to arrange to rent retail premises such as a shop, through an estate agent. Also, it's very likely that a private enterprise agency will agree to your proposed business use, whereas you could run into major planning headaches with shop-type premises. For instance, if people live over it, or it's in a residential area, then you'll have to go to all of the hassle of getting permission for your studio. Also, you'll probably have to maintain an element of sales from any shop premises, as byelaws often require that a shop front should remain a shop front, and not be blanked off. In addition, with a conventional shop, you've got the very real risk of security to worry about. In most private enterprise buildings, there are night guards etc.

So what are the drawbacks of renting a private unit? Well, most companies only want to let them for a limited period—they're not supposed to be your long-term base. That wouldn't be fair on other small businesses looking for space, would it? For this reason, you should beware of investing too heavily in costly fittings that cannot be moved when you leave. For this reason, I would advise that you steer clear of expensive soundproofing treatments. Instead, limit your clients to electronic based musicians—people interested in recording synthesizers and drum machines that you can plug direct into your mixing desk. These won't generate a lot of noise. To further this, you could do much of the monitoring on headphones (Figure 6.1). Working in this way, you'll stand a much better chance of obtaining permission for your studio (wherever you house it).

Working with the electronic fraternity as opposed to the 'thrash thrash' local band will probably enable you to limit much of the equipment necessary to start up—you won't need a drum kit, or the expensive microphones that need to adorn it to get a good sound, and you won't need to spend as much time and effort on acoustic treatments either—a few well placed baffles could be all that's needed to record vocal tracks and the odd acoustic instrument—and you can make baffles cheaply yourself—read Chapter 2 again.

Rates

I feel that you should charge by the hour, and begin charging when the band walks through your door. It's not economical to allow setting-up time/learning how to program a synth time/toilet time/booze breaks etc. Remember, you've got to make some money in your first year whilst you've got a grant to cover you—after that you'll be out on your own. Be fair, but be firm!

Figure 6.1 A recording session need not be nosiy if monitoring is carried out through headphones, with all instruments connected direct to the mixer

I would venture to suggest that you invite prospective clients to your studio for a pre-booking chat. Show them around, demonstrate some recordings, explain your terms, and then if they wish to book time, take a 50% non-refundable deposit from them and issue a receipt. You simply can't devote several hours of one of your working days to a band, only to find that they don't turn up—and you're left twiddling your thumbs when you should, and could have been making money.

How many tracks?

Most bands or potential clients know very little about recording, and the deciding factor, to them, after cost, is usually how many tracks you've got. As we all know, these days, the amount of tracks you have doesn't necessarily directly reflect on the quality of your studio. There are some very bad sixteen track studios around, and some very good four tracks.

Before your caller rings off, you should gently educate them to the fact that much can be achieved with just a few tracks. Explain in simple terms how you can generate more room on the machine by 'bouncing down', and sing the praises of any outboard gear that you've got—if it's good. At this point, you'd also do well to mention your discount and special offer policies, appear helpful, and enquire 'Do our competitors offer you all this?'

Your experience in recording is another plus in your favour. If you've been working in multitrack for a few years, then tell your caller. There are many new studios springing up all over the place, staffed by first-timers who've had no previous experience in engineering. Their only skill to date has been securing a massive bank loan to buy the gear. Good luck to them, but do point out your experience, and promise to do your utmost to achieve a good sound that they, not you, want.

They'll appreciate that, and it'll give them even more justification for using your studio. However, don't give them any bullshit, and don't act aloof—the 'I've got a studio and you haven't' attitude is both unprofessional and uncalled for.

When everything else fails—discounts!

If, after reading Chapter 4—how to sell your services—you are still having trouble, then you're either not trying, or everyone in your area has got short arms and long pockets. In this situation, discounts may be your *only* hope. Even so, it's not a good idea to enter into a price war with your competitors. The best policy is to introduce a comprehensive discount system, and provide special offers when and where possible. One such scheme that I've administered successfully is a recommendation one: A recording client is offered a period of free recording each time they recommend a further customer to the studio for recording. To qualify, this new client must book in for a minimum of four hours, and have paid a non-refundable deposit. This is self-perpetuating, because you can then offer the deal to the new customers, and so on.

Another scheme that works is a voucher promotion. For every four hours that a band is in your studio, you issue a voucher worth a couple of quid. As more vouchers are issued, the free time mounts up, enabling the client to *eventually* have several hours free recording, The key is 'eventually'—this encourages the client to book further sessions to amass more free time instead of going elsewhere. These schemes can easily be adapted to suit all the moneymaking ideas found in Chapter 3.

Music shops can also be extremely useful when touting for business. I persuaded a well-known national music chain to hang little tickets on each of their guitars. This gave the purchaser the chance of some discounted recording. It's best to hang tickets only on the more expensive instruments though. Most people who buy the cheaper models are going to be beginners, and not be recording yet.

7 The business background

Managing the money

Credit accounts

It's surprising how much money you'll have to spend on stock, such as tapes and cassettes. When you first start up, it's often difficult to find the money for these items up front. You're relying on a forthcoming booking to provide working capital. The best way around this problem is to open up a 30 day trade account with a reputable supplier. This will enable you to simply pick up the phone, order your requirements, and arrange for them to be sent more or less immediately. You don't have to pay for the goods until the end of the month. Most firms have special trade account forms that they will be pleased to send you. Normally you'll be required to provide two references before the account can be opened.

Accounts like this can also be opened for another vitally important commodity—advertising space. Without advertising, you won't succeed. Although after a few years you may be able to struggle through on recommendation alone, there are always going to be new musicians in the area who have never heard of you—unless you advertise. It's best to set up a very localized campaign, as most bands won't want to travel out of their own area to record. I've always found that the best means of getting known is through the musical classified section of the local paper—they may also be enticed to give you some editorial too, if you're lucky—and if you spend enough on advertising! See Chapters 4 and 5 for more info.

Set a target

You need to have a plan detailing what you want to achieve. I suggest that you split the year into four, three-monthly quarters, and set a target figure for income in each quarter. Make it realistic—but not too easy. It's fun then striving for target figures—and it's cause for celebration if you exceed them. A business bank account is also a must. These are easily set up, and this makes it easy to split up all your personal purchases / deposits from your business ones—useful when you make tax returns.

Tax

It's important to keep accounts too—and that's something that scares most people off. But it's easy, all you have to do is write down who gives you money, when, what for, and how much. This forms the basis of what you supply to the taxman at the end of the year—or rather, every April. You are allowed to offset earnings against anything that you've spent out, such as stock, heating, lighting, telephone etc.—in fact, almost everything purchased in connection with the running of your business. The difference between the two figures is the amount on which you'll be taxed. Your tax office will give you further information (they're quite friendly people really). If you don't want the hassle of tax returns, then you could engage an accountant.

A sole trader or partnership has to notify the Inspector of Taxes on form 41G that a business has been established. The Inland Revenue have published a useful booklet (IR28), called *Starting In Business*, which can be obtained from your tax office or from the Small Firms Service. If the business makes a profit in its first year, then tax will be payable, although it will not be collected until some time later. However, it's a good idea to put aside some money to meet a possible tax demand as you earn it. Losses may be offset against taxable profits in the following two years.

National Insurance

You'll also need to sort out your own National Insurance contributions. However, if you're not likely to make much money, then you can apply for an exemption certificate. Normally you'll have to fork out for Class 2 contributions—bought as stamps at Post Offices. You can find out more about NI contributions from your local Department of Health and Social Security, there are a number of leaflets dealing with the subject available at these offices. The most useful ones are N41—National Insurance Guide for the Self-Employed, and NI 27—people with Small Earnings from Self Employment (information on exemption certificates).

Setting up a partnership

If you've got a friend who's interested in recording and has some equipment at his disposal—and perhaps some money too—then you may find it worthwhile to set up in business as a partnership. This needn't involve a lot of hassle. All you need to do is visit a bank and apply to open up a joint bank business bank account. To make the money side of things easy to handle, you simply arrange that all cheques must be signed by both parties—that means that neither partner can touch any of the business money without the other's permission—simple. I've got an account like this with the Co-Op bank—they were very helpful.

The only thing to beware of is incompatibility between partners. It's essential that you both get on well, and can reach important decisions quickly and effectively without argument. A word of warning—many friendships are destroyed through business, so be careful!

The insurance maze

Let's get straight to the point—burglars love home recordists, or rather their equipment. Lots of lovely instruments, amps, effects boxes and recording equipment, all left in accessible places like cars and unattended premises—you can imagine the pound signs registering in their eyes as they realise what such equipment is worth on the black market—a sobering thought!

Now that's put the fear of God in you, let's explore ways of minimizing the consequences of such a loss—insurance. Whilst good security systems are also of vital importance, the saying that 'if someone really wants to get in, they will', does unfortunately still ring true. Being adequately covered with an insurance policy not only makes sense, it could save your living or paying hobby from disappearing altogether, should the unthinkable happen.

I thought that it would be straightforward getting cover—just phone up a company and pay the premium—but it's not as easy as all that. The following questions are ones that I felt it necessary to ask when I went insurance shopping recently. They are answered here by a top insurance adviser.

Musical equipment insurance including home studios

I've bought a multitrack recorder and a synthesizer, simply for my own use. I'm not going to take it out of my home. Will such equipment be covered on my existing home contents policy?

Most household contents policies don't specifically cover you for musical instruments. If you want cover for that sort of item, you must advise the insurance company and pay an additional premium—or arrange a separate insurance for those items.

My friend has a guitar, and has come round to do some recording with me for a bit of fun, He accidentally knocks the multitrack off the table and it smashes on the floor. Am I covered?

All risks cover is the norm for musical instruments, and if you have this then you would be able to claim. In theory, you can either claim against your own insurance, or, if there is no cover on that policy, you can claim against your friend's insurance for his negligence. The problem in such cases is that it would come under a small claims court if he denies liability, and you will have to go to a lot of trouble and expense—often more than the item is worth. It's better and easier to have your own insurance cover, and you don't lose friends that way!

Someone phones me up and asks me to record a demo for them which I will be paid for. The client arrives and I do the work. On leaving, I find that my microphone has been stolen. Am I covered?

Check your insurance policy. If anybody pays you for your services then it will be deemed to be a business transaction, and therefore a commercial insurance is required with full theft cover, or larceny. This is where a theft occurs where no violent and forceful entry or exit to the premises can be found. Such cover can be included in a standard contents policy (for private use) as long as you request it at the outset. A good broker will offer you all these options when you take out a policy with him.

On leaving my recording room upstairs, a paying client trips over a rug and falls headlong down the stairs of my house. He threatens to sue me. Am I covered?

Again, if he's actually transacting a business with you then it's a commercial venture. He can take you to court and sue you. If it is found that you are responsible, then your public liability will pick up the claim for the damages. But you still have your own court costs to consider, although these can be insured against with legal expenses cover. Public liability is often included free of charge in many 'package type' insurances for musical and recording equipment.

Adding new equipment to an existing policy

I buy new recording equipment and accessories almost continuously. Do I have to inform my insurance company after every purchase?

No. The way to get around this is to take out adequate insurance cover for the year, making certain that you've got a sufficient sum insured to cover you for any additional purchases during the term. You should effect a maximum loss type cover. i.e., you have £10,000 worth of equipment, but the maximum loss of that equipment may only be £5,000. In the sense that if you had a fire, certain items aren't going to get entirely destroyed.

The main point is to ensure that you have an adequate sum insured of a sufficient maximum single item limit. So, if you took a £10,000, limit, look around you, find out what your equipment is worth and advise that the maximum of any one article within that sum would be, for example, £2,500. That way you're covered for the year as long as no item that you subsequently buy exceeds this total.

Most companies are looking for simplicity to cut their costs. They'll ask you for a list of items that go over a certain limit. However, what they don't want to find is that you're only insuring for 50% of your property. The small print on your policy may have a term known as 'average' applying to it, whereby if you have only got 50% of the correct sum insured, they may only give you 50% of the amount that you've claimed. Most insurance companies are pretty fair though, they realise that you may make additional acquisitions and neglect to advise them. All they're really asking is that you keep relatively up to date within about 15%.

Speed of claims

How long am I likely to have to wait in the event of a claim?

It depends on the type of claim. If someone breaks in and steals your multitrack which you're insured for, and it's a straightforward claim, the insurance companies tend to be pretty quick. Most claims of this nature are dealt with in about a month or so, often quicker.

However, if there is some dubious point on a claim, or there is a problem of third party—such as liability claims—things do tend to drag on. Most brokers will chase the claim and act on your behalf. But, the broker's function is to simply place the business for you at the cover that you've requested, point out the markets to you and locate the best deal. For that he is paid a commission. Most brokers undertake to provide additional services for which they're not getting paid in the field of claims settlement and advice on claims.

Your legal expenses

Some brokers will recommend that you take out legal expenses insurance in various forms (mentioned earlier). This would automatically provide you with solicitors and advice in a difficult claim situation. Most brokers will act on their client's behalf to an extent . It's worth asking how far the broker is willing to go when you take out the policy with him.

Reputable ones will even put the services that they offer to their clients down in writing.

Fires

I wire up my equipment incorrectly and it causes a fire. Can I still claim on insurance?

As long as you have a fire insurance then yes. Obviously if it is deliberate then you aren't covered—It's known as arson and it becomes a police matter. As long as the loss can be deemed to be an insurable incident then there will be a claim payable on the policy.

Home security requirements

Do I have to have special locks and/or a burglar alarm fitted to my home?

Various insurers will ask for certain security requirements to be met, and reasonable precautions taken when you vacate the premises. i.e., you lock the windows and doors. It depends on what policy you've got, who the insurers are, and the area that you live in. Some areas are deemed greater risks than others.

My recording and musical equipment has taken over a whole room of my house—which I call my studio. If I use it simply for my own use, do I have to insure the 'studio' separately?

As mentioned earlier, musical equipment is a special case. This is because most people don't specifically have this 'thief attractive' equipment in their home. Sometimes items can be placed on a contents policy—but it may have to be a specialist one.

Making money from your music

If I am commissioned to do, for example, radio jingles for payment, do I suddenly have to insure my studio room as a business premises—even though clients never actually come directly onto the property?

You are still transacting a business in the eyes of the insurers. Your home contents policy does not cover that. You are acting as a commercial enterprise and therefore you must effect the right commercial policy. Any business at all that is transacted from home, however small, should be okayed with your insurance company. If you don't check and you have a claim, even a domestic one, you may find that they refuse to honour it.

Public liability

What is public liability cover?

This indemnifies any damage that you do to a third party, both personal injury and property damage. You don't have to effect a commercial insurance to get this cover—it is available on its own. A normal house contents insurance will normally cover you, your home and your family for personal liability—the dog biting the postman and so on. But if you are transacting a business then the claim comes under commercial insurance.

Different risks

What are the different elements of risk cover available?

On a standard contents policy, you are normally insured against fire and perils. That's loss as a result of theft and vandalism, storm, burst pipes, earthquake, subsidence and items dropping from the sky. You can then go on to include cover for accidental damage, or all risks. Accidental damage is exactly what it says—the dog chewing the microphone, the wife dusting and knocking over a tape deck etc. All risks is deemed to be literally any loss or damage whatsoever to an insured item. All risks insurance does tend to give you the cover where most of the claims occur. You can specify those particular items within your property on this more expensive cover.

Keeping equipment in the garage

I have decided to convert my detached brick built garage into a studio to avoid annoying the family. Does this affect my insurance?—the garage is within my garden, just a few feet from the house.

You must point this out to your insurers at the time of taking out the insurance. If you do that, then they will take it into consideration when they assess the risk, and quote for it accordingly. In the main though, property is covered under your house contents policy within the boundaries of your overall property. Normally the insurers will ask you detailed questions about the construction of the property, and sometimes come and see it for themselves depending on the area in which you live in and the sum insured involved.

Sometimes I take musical equipment out of the garage and use it in the house—is it still covered?

Point out to your insurers that there will be exchange of equipment between the areas of the property. Some of them will deem such movement as being 'away from the premises', and this may affect your cover. It causes most problems when you've got two separate policies—a business one for the garage, and a normal house contents one for the home with a different company.

In contrast, if a single insurer has covered you under a normal contents policy and noted that equipment is normally kept in the garage then you would be covered—but not if you're making money from it! Things are made more complicated because generally contents insurers will often not wish to take on business cover.

Equipment stolen at gigs

I was asked to record a group live in concert. I took some recording equipment to the venue. Some of it was stolen. Can I claim?

Check that your policy covers you for 'temporary removal of equipment from the insured address'. Some companies will offer you cover, but it does depend on the company. Often you will be asked what you're going to be doing with the equipment at the outset. They will sometimes place exclusions on the policy—such as allowing equipment to be used in the UK, Western Europe, or worldwide. On some normal contents policies you do have the necessary cover to operate in this way, as long as you aren't transacting a business, but you should arrange for it at the outset.

A good broker will ask you all of these relevant questions when he first gets in contact with you. Only then will he be able to truthfully place you with the best company for your needs. Beware of dumb brokers!

Most brokers are not keen to advise me about my studio and equipment, why?

There are various types of brokers and intermediaries, and most tend to specialize in certain areas. Often you'll find that the broker doesn't have a particular company on his agency list that contracts such business. He may not have come across this problem in the past, he may not even wish to contract your sort of business—it may not be financially viable for him. Certain large brokerages have a minimum premium below which they don't wish to deal. Also, there are local brokers who only wish to deal with high volume business, such as car insurance.

A sample equipment quote

As an example, suppose I want to insure a multitrack tape recorder worth about £1200. How much is it likely to cost?

My quote is £31.50 for all risks, but excluding loss from an unattended vehicle. £61.50 including such loss if the vehicle isn't alarmed, and £37.50 if it does have an alarm. However, such quotations do depend to an extent on the area in which you live. This one was for someone in Southampton, England.

Why use a broker

The advantage of using a broker is that, in the event of a claim, they will act as a buffer between you and the insurance company itself. Their job is not only to sell you the policy, but to look after you when you need to claim. A good broker will take all of the worry from your shoulders and liaise with the insurance company and any third parties that may be involved. The services of a broker are entirely free; they get their money from commission on the policies that they sign up.

About claims

The best brokers will be confident enough about their policies to instruct the client to arrange for immediate repair or replacement of equipment. This puts the broker on the spot, because if the insurance company refuses to pay out, then the broker is liable. If he's reputable though, and really does know his policies inside out, then he will be happy to act in this way. If you deal direct with an insurance company then you will often be faced with at least a month's wait in the event of a claim, and a lot of difficult technical communication.

Whatever the difficulties that you experience with your insurance, make sure you get it right! Without it you could end up unable to function as a recording engineer at all. Your first few bookings should more than cover the cost of a suitable policy.

8 The end of the beginning

Well, I've told you everything I know, given you all my ideas, shown how to sell yourself and your services, and made you enemies with your neighbours for life. *Now it's up to you!* Put everything in this book into action, and make recording work for you. It's hard work, but it beats a day job! I would wish you good luck, but after reading this book, you shouldn't need it. Instead, I'll just say—*Go for it!!!*

9 Appendix

Useful addresses

Cassette duplication
Channel 5 Audio, 14 Centre Way, London N9 (Tel 01 803 9036)

Cops, Kent House, Station Approach, Beckenham, Kent (Tel 01 778 8556)

Duplitape, 37 Shaw Road, Heaton Moor, Stockport, Cheshire (Tel 061 442 6910)

Enterprise Music Ltd, Moss Industrial Estate, Leigh, Lancs (Tel 0942 260175)

Fairview Music, Great Gutter Lane, Willerby, Hull HU10 6EP (Tel 0482 653116)

KG Engineering, Oak Place, Newton Abbot, Devon,TQ12 2EX (Tel 0626 64054)

Magnetic Image Ltd, Ladbroke Grove, London W10 (Tel 01 968 8848)

Manchester Tapeline, 53 Corporation Road, Audenshaw, Manchester (Tel 061 336 5438)

Martlett, Thrist House, Wellington Place, Hastings, Sussex (Tel 0424 443805)

Mirror Cassettes, Basement, 346 North End Road, Fulham SW6 (Tel 01 385 1816)

RMS, 43 Clifton Road, London SE25 6PX (Tel 01 653 4965)

Simon Stable, 20 West End, Launton, Bicester OX6 ODF (Tel 0869 252831)

Street Copy, 1/3 Berry Street, London EC1 (Tel 01 251 3924)

The Studio, Kent House Approach, Beckenham, Kent BR3 1JD (Tel 01 778 8556)

Studio Republic, 17 High Street, Pinner (Tel 01 866 5555)

Surrey Sound/Solo Sound, 70 Kingston Road, Leatherhead, Surrey (Tel 372 379444)

WME, Warwick Chambers, 14 Corporation Street, Birmingham (Tel 021 643 7113)

Magazines (UK)
Blues and Soul, 153 Praed Street, London W2.

British Music Yearbook, 241 Shaftesbury Avenue, London WC2H 8EH.

Country Music Round Up, 32 286-287 High Street, Upper Precinct, Lincoln LN2 1AL.

Disco and Club Trade International, 410 St John Street, London EC1.

Guitarist, Alexander House, Forehill, Ely, Cambridge CB7 4AF.

Home Keyboard Review, Alexander House, Forehill, Ely, Cambridge CB7 4AF.

Home & Studio Recording, Alexander House, Forehill, Ely, Cambridge CB7 4AF.

International Musician, Cover Publications, Northern and Shell Building, PO Box 381, Mill Harbour, London E14 9TW.

In Tune, 81 Gloucester Street, London SW1V 4EB.

JOCKS, Spotlight Publications, Greater London House, Hampstead Road, London NW1 7QZ.

Kerrang, Spotlight Publications, Greater London House, Hampstead Road, London NW1 7QZ.

Keyboard Player, Tileyard House, 18 Tileyard Road, York Way, London N7 9AN.

Making Music, Track Record Publishing, 40 Bowling Green Lane, London EC1R 0NE.

Melody Maker, Kings Reach Tower, Stamford Street, London SE1 9LS.

Music Technology, Alexander House, Forehill, Ely, Cambridge CB7 4AF.

Music Week, Spotlight Publications, Greater London House, Hampstead Road, London NW1 7QZ.

New Musical Express, Kings Reach Tower, Stamford Street, London SE1 9LS.

No 1, Kings Reach Tower, Stamford Street, London SE1 9LS.

Record Mirror, Spotlight Publications, Greater London House, Hampstead Road, London NW1 7QZ.

Rhythm, Alexander House, Forehill, Ely, Cambridge CB7 4AF.

Smash Hits, 52-55 Carnaby Street, London W1V 1PF.

Sound on Sound, PO Box 30, St Ives, Cambs PE17 4XQ.

Sounds, Spotlight Publications, Greater London House, Hampstead Road, London NW1 7QZ.

Studio Sound, Link House, Dingwall Ave, Croydon CR9 2TA.

Studio Week, Spotlight Publications, Greater London House, Hampstead Road, London NW1 7QZ.

What Keyboard? Cover Publications, Northern and Shell Building, PO Box 381, Mill Harbour, London E14 9TW.

Yamaha Xpress, Mount Avenue, Bletchley, Milton Keynes MK1 1JE.

Magazines (USA and Canada)
Canadian Musician, 832 Mount Pleasant Road, Toronto, Ontario M4P 2L3.

Electronic Musician Magazine, 260B Ninth Street, Berkeley, CA 94710.

International Musician, Suite 600, Paramount Building, 1501 Broadway, NY 10036.

Keyboard, 20085 Stevens Creek, Cupertino, CA 95014.

Mix Magazine, 260B Ninth Street, Berkeley, CA 94710.

Modern Drummer, 870 Pompton Avenue, Cedar Grove, New Jersey 07009.

Music, Computers and Software, 190 East Main Street, Huntingdon, NY.

Music & Sound Output, 25 Willowdale Avenue, Port Washington, NY 11050

Music Technology, 7361 Topanga Canyon Blvd. Ganoga Park CA 91303.

Musician, 1515 Broadway, 39th Floor, NY 10036.

Percussion, 6 Avenue J, Brooklyn, NY 11230.

Manufacturers (UK)
Akai, Electronic Music Division, Haslemere Heathrow Estate, Silver Jubilee Way, Parkway, Hounslow, Middx TW4 6NQ (Tel 01-897 6388).

AKG, Vienna Court, Catteshaw Lane, Godalming, Surrey GU7 1JG.

Beyer Dynamic, Unit 14, Cliffe Industrial Estate, Lewes,

Sussex BN8 6JL (Tel 0273 479411).

Bose UK, Trinity Trading Estate, Sittingbourne, Kent M10 2PD (Tel 0795 75341).

Casio Electronics Co Limited, Unit 6, 1000 North Circular Road, London NW2 7JD (Tel 01-450 9131).

Electromusic Research, 14 Mount Close, Wickford, Essex SS11 8HG (Tel 0702 335747).

Elka-Orla UK, 3/5 Fourth Avenue, Bluebridge Ind Estate, Halstead, Essex C09 2SY (Tel 0787 475325).

Emu Systems, Syco, Conduit Place, London W2 (Tel 01-724 2451).

Ensoniq UK, PO Box 806, London NW3 1HZ (Tel 01-435 2434).

Farfisa UK, Fraser Street, Burnley, Lancs BB1 1UL (Tel 0282 35431).

Harman Audio (UK), Mill Street, Slough, Berks SL2 5DD (Tel 0753 76911).

John Hornby Skewes, Salem House, Garforth, Leeds LS25 1PX (Tel 0532 865381).

Kawai UK, Windebank House, 2 Durley Road, Bournemouth BH2 5JJ (Tel 0202 296629).

Korg UK, 8-9 The Crystal Centre, Elm Grove Road, Harrow, Middx HA1 2YR (Tel 01-427 5377).

Oberheim, 6 Letchworth Business Centre, Avenue 1, Letchworth, Herts SG6 2HR (Tel 0462 480000).

Roland (UK) Limited, Great West Trading Estate, 983 Great West Road, Brentford, Middx (Tel 01-568 4578).

Rosetti, 138 Old Street, London EC1V 9BL.

Sequential Inc, PO Box 16, 3640 AA Midjdtrecht, The Netherlands.

Simmons, Alan Park, Hatfield Road, St Albans, Herts AL4 OJH

Steinberg Research, The Studio, Church Street, Stonesfield OX7 2PS (Tel 099389 228).

Tannoy, The Bilton Centre, Coronation Road, High Wycombe, Bucks HP12 3SB (Tel 0494 450606).

Technics, 300 Bath Road, Slough Berks SL1 6JB (Tel 0753 34522).

Yamaha, Mount Avenue, Bletchley, Milton Keynes MK1 1JE (Tel 0908 71771).

Other organisations (UK)
Akai Active, Haslemere Heathrow Estate, Silver Jubilee Way, Parkway, Hounslow, Middx TW4 6NQ (Tel 01-897 6388).

Casio MIDI User's Club, Unit 6, 1000 North Circular Road, London NW2 7JD (Tel 01-450 9131).

Mirage User Group, 2 Walnut Tree Cottages, The Green, Frant, E Sussex TN3 9DE.

Roland Newslink, Roland (UK), Great West Trading Estate, 983 Great West Road, Brentford, Middx (Tel 01-568 4578).

Steinberg User Club, 68 Wilsdon Way, Kidlington, Oxford OX5 1TX.

Yamaha X Club, Mount Avenue, Bletchley, Milton Keynes MK1 1JE (Tel 0908 78894).

Manufacturers (USA)
Akai Professional, PO Box 2344, Fort Worth, Texas, TX 76113.

Alesis, PO Box 3908, Los Angeles, CA 90078.

Casio, 15 Gardner Road, Fairfield, NJ 07006.

EMU Systems, 1600 Green Hills Road, Scotts Valley, CA 95066.

Ensoniq, 155 Great Valley Parkway, Malvern, PA 19355.

Fairlight, 2945 Westwood Blvd., Los Angeles, CA 90064.

Fostex, 15431 Blackburn Ave, Norwalk, CA 90650.

Kawai America, 2055 East University Drive, PO Box 9045, Compton, CA 90224.

Korg USA, 89 Frost Street, Westbury, NY 11590.

Kurzweil Music Systems, 411 Waverley Oaks Road, Waltham, MA 02154.

Oberheim, 11650 W Olympic Blvd. Los Angeles, CA 90064.

RolandCorp US, 7200 Dominion Circle, Los Angeles, CA 90040.

Sequential Circuits Inc, 3051 North First Street, San Jose, CA 95134.

Simmons USA, 23917 Craftsman Road, Calabassas, CA 91302.

Yamaha PO Box 6600, Buena Park, CA 90622.

Other organisations (USA)
International MIDI Assocation, 11857 Hartsook Street, North Hollywood, CA 91607.

MIDI Manufacturer's Association, c/o RolandCorp US, 7200 Dominion Circle Los Angeles, CA 90040.

Roland User Group, c/o RolandCorp US, 7200 Dominion Circle, Los Angeles, CA 90040.

Index

photocopy, 41, 42
photographer, 43
pillows and cushions, 12
pinch roller, 26
pitch control, 54
planning your studio, 1
playback, 18, 64
portable multitracker, 37
postage charges, 32
postcard campaign, 39
post-production work, 37
powerful bass, 21
pre-booking chat, 80
pressing plant, 46
press releases, 74
prices, 31, 35, 47
price war, 81
printing, 30, 51, 57, 60
private customers, 33, 36
private enterprise schemes, 78
psychoacoustic enhancement, 21
public liability, 77, 86, 89
public relations, 71, 75
punchy sound, 22

radio, 21, 58, 71, 72, 89
rates, 79
readership survey sheet, 72
real time copying, 28
recommendation, 81, 83
recording level, 3, 15
record pressing, 46
record pressing plants, 59
record shops, 57
reference book of e.q. settings, 23
rehearsal recording, 38
renting, 79
reverberation, 21, 46, 63
ribbon mic, 24
room tuning, 23

sale or return, 57
sales incentive, 52
salesmen, 58
sales outlets, 42
sales target, 83
sample equipment insurance quote, 91
sampler, 19, 50
second generation, 18
secondhand ¼ inch machines, 19

selling your cassettes, 57
sell yourself - on cassette, 56
send and receive, 19
sequencer, 19, 63-65
setting up a partnership, 85
shop-type premises, 79
side labels, 31
signal leads, 46
signal processors, 16
signal to noise ratio, 15
Small Firms Service, 84
solo recordings, 12
sound, 77
sound attenuator, 10
sound dampener for the ceiling, 4
sound on sound, 63
soundproofing, 4, 79
Sounds magazine, 32
speakers, 12, 65
specialist newspapers, 55
stands for the mics, 19
stereo cassette deck, 18
stereo image, 18, 22
stereo recorder, 50
stop-foil, 34
strip lighting, 13
submixes, 54
supplementary benefit, 78
suppliers, 72
synthesizer, 63, 85, 79

Tandy, 35, 34
tape care, 27
tape hiss, 14
tape quality, 14
tape/slide presentation, 62
tape transport, 26
target audience, 72
tax, 77, 84
TDK SAX, 14, 57
teaching, 39
telephone answering machines, 32
tell - show - tel, 70
theme music, 51
thickening vocal sounds, 20
tone considerations, 15
tone controls, 17
trade account, 83
travelling expenses, 37, 47
treble, 15
tuition tapes, 40